BAPTISTWAY AD[...]
LARGE PRINT EDITION

The Gospel of John
BELIEVE IN JESUS AND LIVE!

PAM GIBBS
RONNY MARRIOTT
WESLEY SHOTWELL
DIANNE SWAIM

BAPTISTWAYPRESS®
Dallas, Texas

The Gospel of John: Believe in Jesus and Live!—
BaptistWay Adult Bible Study Guide®—Large Print Edition

Copyright © 2014 by BAPTISTWAY PRESS®.
All rights reserved.
Printed in the United States of America.

No part of this book may be used or reproduced in any manner whatsoever without written permission except in the case of brief quotations. For information, contact BAPTISTWAY PRESS, Baptist General Convention of Texas, 333 North Washington, Dallas, TX 75246-1798.

BAPTISTWAY PRESS® is registered in U.S. Patent and Trademark Office.

Unless otherwise indicated, all Scripture quotations in lessons 1–6, 10–12, and the Christmas lesson are taken from the HOLY BIBLE, NEW INTERNATIONAL VERSION®. Copyright © 1973, 1978, 1984 Biblica. Used by permission of Zondervan. All rights reserved. NIV84 refers to this edition of the New International Version.

Unless otherwise indicated, all Scripture quotations in lessons 7–9 are taken from the New Revised Standard Version Bible, copyright 1989, Division of Christian Education of the National Council of the Churches of Christ in the United States of America. Used by permission. All rights reserved.

All Scripture quotations marked NASB are taken from the 1995 update of the New American Standard Bible®, Copyright © The Lockman Foundation 1960, 1962, 1963, 1968, 1971, 1972, 1973, 1975, 1977, 1995. Used by permission. NASB refers to this edition of the New American Standard Bible®.

BAPTISTWAY PRESS® Leadership Team
Executive Director, Baptist General Convention of Texas: David Hardage
Director, Church Ministry Resources: Chris Liebrum
Director, Bible Study/Discipleship Team: Phil Miller
Publisher, BaptistWay Press®: Scott Stevens

Cover and Interior Design and Production: Desktop Miracles, Inc.
Printing: Data Reproductions Corporation

First edition: December 2014
ISBN-13: 978-1-938355-28-8

How to Make the Best Use of This Issue

Whether you're the teacher or a student—

1. Start early in the week before your class meets.

2. Overview the study. Review the table of contents and read the study introduction. Try to see how each lesson relates to the overall study.

3. Use your Bible to read and consider prayerfully the Scripture passages for the lesson. (You'll see that each writer has chosen a favorite translation for the lessons in this issue. You're free to use the Bible translation you prefer and compare it with the translation chosen for that unit, of course.)

4. After reading all the Scripture passages in your Bible, then read the writer's comments. The comments are intended to be an aid to your study of the Bible.

5. Read the small articles—"sidebars"—in each lesson. They are intended to provide additional, enrichment information and inspiration and to encourage thought and application.

6. Try to answer for yourself the questions included in each lesson. They're intended to encourage further

thought and application, and they can also be used in the class session itself.

If you're the teacher—

A. Do all of the things just mentioned, of course. As you begin the study with your class, be sure to find a way to help your class know the date on which each lesson will be studied. You might do this in one or more of the following ways:

B. In the first session of the study, briefly overview the study by identifying for your class the date on which each lesson will be studied. Lead your class to write the date in the table of contents on page 11 and on the first page of each lesson.

- Make and post a chart that indicates the date on which each lesson will be studied.

- Send your class members a text or e-mail with the dates the lessons will be studied.

- Provide a bookmark with the lesson dates. You may want to include information about your church and then use the bookmark as an outreach tool, too. A model for a bookmark can be downloaded from www.baptistwaypress.org on the Adults—Bible Studies page.

- Develop a sticker with the lesson dates, and place it on the table of contents or on the back cover.

How to Make the Best Use of This Issue   5

- • Get a copy of the *Teaching Guide*, a companion piece to this *Study Guide*. The *Teaching Guide* contains additional Bible comments plus two teaching plans. The teaching plans in the *Teaching Guide* are intended to provide practical, easy-to-use teaching suggestions that will work in your class.

C. After you've studied the Bible passage, the lesson comments, and other material, use the teaching suggestions in the *Teaching Guide* to help you develop your plan for leading your class in studying each lesson.

D. Teaching resource items for use as handouts are available free at www.baptistwaypress.org.

E. Additional Bible study comments on the lessons are available online. Call 1–866–249–1799 or e-mail baptistway@texasbaptists.org to order *Premium Adult Online Bible Commentary*. It is available only in electronic format (PDF) from our website, www.baptistwaypress.org. The price of these comments for the entire study is $6 for individuals and $25 for a group of five. A church or class that participates in our advance order program for free shipping can receive the *Premium Adult Online Bible Commentary* free. Call 1–866–249–1799 or see www.baptistwaypress.org to purchase or for information on participating in our free shipping program for the next study.

F. Additional teaching plans are also available in electronic format (PDF) by calling 1–866–249–1799. The price of these additional teaching plans for the entire study is $5 for an individual and $20 for a group of five. A church or class that participates in our advance order program for free shipping can receive *Premium Adult Online Teaching Plans* free. Call 1–866–249–1799 or see www.baptistwaypress.org for information on participating in our free shipping program for the next study.

G. You also may want to get the enrichment teaching help that is provided on the Internet by the *Baptist Standard* at www.baptiststandard.com. (Other class participants may find this information helpful, too.) The *Baptist Standard* is available online for an annual subscription rate of $10. Subscribe online at www.baptiststandard.com or call 214–630–4571. (A free thirty-day trial subscription is currently available.)

H. Enjoy leading your class in discovering the meaning of the Scripture passages and in applying these passages to their lives.

Do you use a Kindle?

This BaptistWay *Adult Bible Study Guide* plus *14 Habits of Highly Effective Disciples; Guidance for the Seasons of Life; Living Generously for Jesus' Sake; Profiles in Character; Psalms: Songs from the Heart of Faith; Amos, Hosea, Isaiah, Micah; Jeremiah and Ezekiel; The Gospel of Matthew; The Gospel of Mark; The Gospel of Luke: Jesus' Personal Touch; The Gospel of John: Part One; The Gospel of John: Part Two; The Book of Acts: Time to Act on Acts 1:8; The Corinthian Letters: Imperatives for an Imperfect Church; Hebrews and the Letters of Peter;* and *Letters to the Ephesians and Timothy* are now available in a Kindle edition. The easiest way to find these materials is to search for "BaptistWay" on your Kindle or go to www.amazon.com/kindle and do a search for "BaptistWay." The Kindle edition can be studied not only on a Kindle but also on a PC, Mac, iPhone, iPad, Blackberry, or Android phone using the Kindle app available free from amazon.com/kindle.

AUDIO BIBLE STUDY LESSONS

Do you want to use your walk/run/ride, etc. time to study the Bible? Or maybe you're looking for a way to study the Bible when you just can't find time to read? Or maybe you know someone who has difficulty seeing to read even our *Large Print Study Guide*?

Then try our audio Bible study lessons, available on *Living Generously for Jesus' Sake; Profiles in Character; Amos, Hosea, Isaiah, Micah; The Gospel of Matthew; The Gospel of Mark; The Gospel of Luke; The Gospel of John: Part One; The Gospel of John: Part Two; The Book of Acts; The Corinthian Letters; Galatians and 1 & 2 Thessalonians;* and *The Letters of James and John*. For more information or to order, call 1–866–249–1799 or e-mail baptistway@texasbaptists.org. The files are downloaded from our website. You'll need an audio player or phone that plays MP3 files (like an iPod®, but many MP3 players are available), or you can listen on a computer.

Writers for This Study Guide

Pam Gibbs wrote **lessons one through four**. Pam is a freelance writer and speaker who lives in Nashville, Tennessee, where she serves as the youth minister at Bellevue Baptist Church. A native Texan, Pam is a graduate of Southwestern Baptist Theological Seminary and has been involved in ministry for over twenty years. She loves spending time with her husband Jim and daughter Kaitlyn.

Wesley Shotwell wrote **lessons five and six and the Christmas lesson.** Wesley is the pastor of Ash Creek Baptist Church, Azle, Texas. Dr. Shotwell formerly was pastor of churches in Tennessee. He is a graduate of Baylor University (B.A.), Southwestern Baptist Theological Seminary (M.Div.), and Vanderbilt Divinity School (D.Min.).

Dianne Swaim wrote **lessons seven through nine.** Dianne is a chaplain at the Veterans Administration Hospital in Little Rock, Arkansas. She is a graduate of Southwestern Baptist Theological Seminary (M.Div.). She served as the Spiritual Care Manager for Arkansas Hospice, retiring in

2012. In addition to serving as a fee-basis chaplain, she is a speaker and free-lance writer. She lives with her husband Gordon in North Little Rock, Arkansas.

Ronny Marriott wrote **lessons ten through twelve**. Dr. Marriott is pastor of First Baptist Church, Temple, Texas. He holds the Doctor of Ministry degree from Southwestern Baptist Theological Seminary.

The Gospel of John: Believe in Jesus and Live!

How to Make the Best Use of This Issue	3
Writers for This Study Guide	9
Introducing The Gospel of John: Believe in Jesus and Live!	13

DATE OF STUDY

UNIT ONE
Jesus' Public Ministry (3+ Years)

LESSON 1	_____	*In Him Was Life* JOHN 1:1–18	24
LESSON 2	_____	*You Must Be Born Again* JOHN 3:1–21	38
LESSON 3	_____	*The Bread of Life* JOHN 6:25–51	52
LESSON 4	_____	*The Truth Will Set You Free* JOHN 8:31–47	68
LESSON 5	_____	*Life to the Full* JOHN 10:1–21	82
LESSON 6	_____	*The Resurrection and the Life* JOHN 11:17–44	96

UNIT TWO

Jesus' Private Ministry (3+ Days)

LESSON 7	_____	*The Full Extent of His Love* JOHN 13:1–17; 31–38	**114**
LESSON 8	_____	*The Way, the Truth, and the Life* JOHN 14:1–14	**130**
LESSON 9	_____	*Apart From Me You Can Do Nothing* JOHN 15:1–17	**144**
LESSON 10	_____	*It is Finished* JOHN 19:28–42	**160**
LESSON 11	_____	*Stop Doubting and Believe* JOHN 20:10–31	**174**
LESSON 12	_____	*Follow Me!* JOHN 21:1–25	**188**
CHRISTMAS LESSON	_____	*Nothing Is Impossible with God* LUKE 1:26–45	**204**

Our Next New Study	**217**
How to Order More Bible Study Materials	**219**

Introducing

THE GOSPEL OF JOHN:
Believe in Jesus and Live!

Approaching This Study of the Gospel of John

We live in a skeptical society. Whether the messages we receive come through marketing efforts designed to influence our purchase decisions or explanations from political, entertainment, or religious figures mired in scandal, we are slow to believe. Think about it. What does it require for someone to convince you that their message is true?

The Apostle John wrote his Gospel to convince people to believe in Jesus and live! In fact, he used the Greek word translated "believe" ninety-eight times in his writing.[1] The purpose of his Gospel is summed up in the following verses:

"Jesus did many other miraculous signs in the presence of his disciples, which are not recorded in this book. But these are written that you may believe that Jesus is the Christ, the Son of God, and that by believing you may have life in his name" (John 20:30–31).[2]

The type of belief John writes about is more than mental agreement with a set of facts. It is accepting truth as truth[3], but even more importantly, it is placing confidence, faith, and trust in the person who embodies those truths. To believe in Jesus is to accept his words as truth and to place our total dependence on him for our lives, both for time and eternity.

And what sort of life does John write about? John quotes Jesus as follows, ". . . I have come that they may have life, and have it to the full" (John 10:10). The Greek word translated "life" in this verse refers to life in the spirit and soul, and most often speaks of eternal life.[4] John wants his readers to know that amazing, abundant, eternal life is available to all who will place their faith and trust in Jesus.

Since the beginning of our BaptistWay Bible study series, we have focused on the Gospel of John three times previously. (This particular study appears in our fourteenth year of publishing ongoing curriculum.) Each of these studies—this one as well as the previous three—is different from the others in its approach to the individual lessons.[5]

We think studying Scriptures directly about Jesus on a regular basis is important, so we provide a study of a Gospel each year. Each study begins with a new emphasis and fresh outlines and lessons are created.

A Little Background on the Gospel of John

The Gospel of John was written in a different manner than the synoptic Gospels (Matthew, Mark, and Luke.) John did not write an historical account of the life of Jesus but rather a "powerful argument for the incarnation, a conclusive demonstration that Jesus was, and is, the very heaven-sent Son of God, and the only source of eternal life."[6] This Gospel is more theological in nature focusing on revelation and redemption. John gave attention to key events in Jesus' life and ministry and took time to explain and apply their meaning.

John, the author of this Gospel, was one of the "Sons of Thunder" with his brother James, and a son of Zebedee. He was a rough and tumble fisherman who became one of Jesus' inner circle of disciples (with James and Peter), and eventually was given the responsibility to care for Jesus' mother at his crucifixion (John 19:26–27). Scholars place the writing of the Gospel of John somewhere around A.D. 90, with John writing from Ephesus some time after the destruction of Jerusalem in 70 A.D.

This study of the Gospel of John is divided into two areas of focus:

1. Jesus' Public Ministry—a period of roughly three-and-a-half years that consisted of Jesus preaching, teaching, and performing various miracles.

2. Jesus' Private Ministry—a period of roughly a three-and-a-half days during the Passion week as Jesus spent intimate times of instruction, encouragement, preparation, and comfort with his disciples.[7]

The Gospel of John in Our Day

How should John's Gospel impact Jesus' followers today? We live in a world full of people who are searching for truth and meaning and purpose in life. There are many religions and philosophies available to these seekers. The Gospel of John contains the story of the preexistent Savior of the world who became one of us so that we could enjoy the full and abundant life we were created for. We are called to be an extension of the grace and truth of Christ that the world so desperately needs.

John's Gospel provides proof that can encourage and empower us to truly live and to be ambassadors of the light of Christ. May this study empower and encourage us to proclaim the truth that, "God so loved the world that he gave his one and only Son, that whoever believes in him shall not perish but have eternal life. For God did not send his Son into the world to condemn the world, but to save the world through him" (John 3:16–17).

Note: Since the time of the first release of these materials includes the Christmas holiday, a Christmas lesson is included to meet the needs of churches who wish to have an emphasis on Christmas at this time.

UNIT ONE: JESUS' PUBLIC MINISTRY (3+ YEARS)

Lesson 1	In Him Was Life	John 1:1–18
Lesson 2	You Must Be Born Again	John 3:1–21
Lesson 3	The Bread of Life	John 6:25–51
Lesson 4	The Truth Will Set You Free	John 8:31–47
Lesson 5	Life to the Full	John 10:1–21
Lesson 6	The Resurrection and the Life	John 11:17–44

UNIT TWO: JESUS' PRIVATE MINISTRY (3+ DAYS)

Lesson 7	The Full Extent of His Love	John 13:1–17; 31–38
Lesson 8	The Way, the Truth, and the Life	John 14:1–14
Lesson 9	Apart From Me You Can Do Nothing	John 15:1–17
Lesson 10	It is Finished	John 19:28–42
Lesson 11	Stop Doubting and Believe	John 20:10–31
Lesson 12	Follow Me!	John 21:1–25
Christmas Lesson	Nothing Is Impossible with God	Luke 1:26–45

Additional Resources for Studying the *Gospel of John*[8]

Kenneth L. Barker and John R. Kohlenberger III. *The Expositor's Bible Commentary—Abridged Edition: New Testament*. Grand Rapids, Michigan: Zondervan, 1994.

Bruce Barton, Philip Comfort, Grant Osborne, Linda K. Taylor, and Dave Veerman. *Life Application New Testament Commentary*. Carol Stream, Illinois: Tyndale House Publishers, Inc., 2001.

Gary M. Burge. *John*. The NIV Application Commentary. Grand Rapids, Michigan: Zondervan, 2000.

Craig S. Keener. *IVP Bible Background Commentary: New Testament*. Downers Grove, Illinois: InterVarsity Press, 1993.

George R. Beasley-Murray. *John*. Volume 36 of Word Biblical Commentary. Nashville: Nelson Reference & Electronic, 1989.

A.T. Robertson. *Word Pictures in the New Testament: Concise Edition*. Nashville, Tennessee: Holman Bible Publishers, 2000.

Spiros Zodhiates and Warren Baker. *Hebrew-Greek Key Word Study Bible, New International Version*. Grand Rapids, Michigan: Zondervan, 1996.

Charles R. Swindoll. *Insights on John—Swindoll's New Testament Insights*. Grand Rapids, Michigan: Zondervan, 2010.

NOTES

1. Charles R. Swindoll, *Swindoll's New Testament Insights: Insights on John* (Grand Rapids, MI: Zondervan, 2010), 17.
2. Unless otherwise indicated, all Scripture quotations in "Introducing the Gospel of John: Believe in Jesus and Live!" are from the New International Version (1984 edition).
3. Swindoll, 17.
4. Spiros Zodhiates and Warren Baker, *Hebrew-Greek Key Word Study Bible, New International Version* (Grand Rapids, MI: Zondervan, 1996), 1630.
5. See www.baptistwaypress.org.
6. Bruce Barton, Philip Comfort, Grant Osborne, Linda K. Taylor, and Dave Veerman, *Life Application New Testament Commentary* (Carol Stream, Il: Tyndale House Publishers, Inc., 2001), 365.
7. Swindoll, 19.
8. Listing a book does not imply full agreement by the writers or BAPTISTWAY PRESS® with all of its comments.

UNIT ONE
Jesus' Public Ministry (3+ Years)

Unit One, "Jesus' Public Ministry" contains six lessons covering events that occurred during Jesus' public ministry. In these lessons we see Jesus preaching, teaching, and performing miracles. Lesson one sets a deep theological tone as John describes the preexistent Savior who became flesh and dwelt among us. Lesson two records Jesus' conversation with Nicodemus as he explained his purpose and the need to be born again. In lesson three Jesus uses the background of his miraculous feeding of the 5,000 to talk about how he can meet our deepest spiritual hunger. Lesson four focuses on how we can be freed from sin to follow God and lesson five speaks about the abundant life that is available in Jesus. Lesson six reveals both Jesus' compassion and his resurrection power!

UNIT ONE: JESUS' PUBLIC MINISTRY (3+ YEARS)

Lesson 1	In Him Was Life	John 1:1–18
Lesson 2	You Must Be Born Again	John 3:1–21
Lesson 3	The Bread of Life	John 6:25–51
Lesson 4	The Truth Will Set You Free	John 8:31–47
Lesson 5	Life to the Full	John 10:1–21
Lesson 6	The Resurrection and the Life	John 11:17–44

FOCAL TEXT
John 1:1–18

BACKGROUND
John 1:1–18

LESSON ONE
In Him Was Life

MAIN IDEA

Jesus Christ, the Word made flesh, is eternal and is the source of eternal life.

QUESTION TO EXPLORE

What is Jesus' true identity?

STUDY AIM

To comprehend Jesus' unique identity and to help others recognize him for whom he truly is

QUICK READ

This passage, also known as "The Prologue," is a summary of the entire Gospel of John. It tells us that God became a living, breathing person (Christ) in order to redeem humanity from its sin.

Introduction

Have you ever eaten a dessert (or even an entrée) that was so good you were disappointed when it was gone? Perhaps a fancy creation from a restaurant left you longing for more. In a way, today's Scripture will leave you with that same feeling. The opening verses of the Book of John are so rich in theology and meaning. Studying it for only a few moments will merely scratch the surface of this powerful proclamation of the gospel. You will long for more.[1]

JOHN 1:1–18

1 In the beginning was the Word, and the Word was with God, and the Word was God. **2** He was with God in the beginning.

3 Through him all things were made; without him nothing was made that has been made. **4** In him was life, and that life was the light of men. **5** The light shines in the darkness, but the darkness has not understood it.

6 There came a man who was sent from God; his name was John. **7** He came as a witness to testify concerning that light, so that through him all men might believe. **8** He himself was not the light; he came only as a witness to the light. **9** The true light that gives light to every man was coming into the world.

LESSON 1: *In Him Was Life*

10 He was in the world, and though the world was made through him, the world did not recognize him. **11** He came to that which was his own, but his own did not receive him. **12** Yet to all who received him, to those who believed in his name, he gave the right to become children of God— **13** children born not of natural descent, nor of human decision or a husband's will, but born of God.

14 The Word became flesh and made his dwelling among us. We have seen his glory, the glory of the One and Only, who came from the Father, full of grace and truth.

15 John testifies concerning him. He cries out, saying, "This was he of whom I said, 'He who comes after me has surpassed me because he was before me.'" **16** From the fullness of his grace we have all received one blessing after another. **17** For the law was given through Moses; grace and truth came through Jesus Christ. **18** No one has ever seen God, but God the One and Only, who is at the Father's side, has made him known.

The Beginning of It All (1:1–5)

Notice that the first few words in the Gospel of John parallel the opening words of the book of Genesis. While Genesis focuses on God the Father being present before creation, John 1:1 focuses on the Word (which we find out later is Jesus) being present before creation as well. This verse also equates the Word with God. Verse 2 continues the emphasis of Jesus' preexistence with God. This key truth will play an important role later on as Jesus explains that what he says and does comes from God because he is God. This theme of the intimate relationship between God the Father and God the Son continues on throughout the New Testament (especially in the book of John), even though it remains a mystery to us.

In verse 3, John asserted that not only was Jesus present at creation, but that he created all things. This contradicts the teaching of some religious groups and cults that teach that Jesus was not equal with God, but was the first being created by God. Verse 4 indicates that "life" was found in him. This word is most often connected with describing supernatural life as opposed to biological life, although given the reference to creation in the previous verse the meaning could be taken both ways.

Not only is Jesus the source of life, he is life (John 14:6), and is light as well. Verse 5 tells us that Jesus (as the light) shines in the darkness, which can be understood as a reference to Jesus coming to the earth. He is the light of the world (John 8:12) that even the darkness cannot overcome. The word "overcome" can also mean "comprehend." If understood this way, Jesus was the light directing humanity toward God (and Jesus himself), but the world could not understand (or did not comprehend) his radical message of eternal life through faith and trust in him. Nevertheless, without Jesus we are in darkness, and we are lost.

The darkness of the world can be seen most keenly in today's global events. From fighting within nations and between nations to infanticide and suicide, the world indeed lives in darkness and despair. Yet, there is still hope. Jesus is the same light now as he was then. The Holy Spirit still draws people to Jesus, and we as his followers are charged with the task of being light as well, drawing attention to the ultimate Light (Matthew 5:14–16).

A Witness to the Light (1:6–9)

In these verses, the focus shifts somewhat from Jesus to the forerunner of Jesus, John the Baptist. While these verses do not specifically use the term "the Baptist," other Scriptures fill in the blanks, so to speak, letting the reader know that John the Baptist and the man named John in verse 6 are the same person.

Verses 7–8 describe John's purpose—to testify about the light (Christ) so that people would believe in him. These verses make it clear that John the Baptist was not the Messiah, but was rather the "voice of one crying out in the wilderness: Make straight the way of the Lord" (John 1:23). He understood his role as a herald who was to prepare the people for the coming of Jesus, "the true light . . . coming into the world" (1:9).

The distinction of John as the forerunner of the Messiah was an important one to make. John the Baptist was a very respected and prominent man at the time, and many people came to hear him preach. Many of his hearers were content to follow him and might have followed John as the Messiah rather than Jesus. Later on in the same chapter, John made clear his subservient role to Jesus when he said, "He [Jesus] is the one who comes after me, the thongs of whose sandals I am not worthy to untie" (1:27).

While Christians may not be as radical as John the Baptist in their dress or diet today, they continue John's mission. We, as Jesus' followers, are charged with the task of telling others what Christ has done for us, and about the eternal life he offers. Our words and actions should point others toward a relationship with Jesus. The Messiah has indeed come, and we are proclaimers of that truth.

Belonging by Belief, Not Blood (1:10–13)

These verses shift back to a focus on Jesus. Verse 10 repeats verse 3, but then adds an important note: Although Jesus came into the very world he created, the world—specifically the people in the world—did not recognize or acknowledge Jesus. They could not accept him as the promised Messiah. The rejection was not universal, however, because John went on to talk about those who would

LESSON 1: *In Him Was Life*   31

turn to Christ and receive him. They would become the children of God. This standing as God's beloved would cause conflict with the religious Jews who claimed to be God's favored ones (namely, the religious leaders).

In verse 12, the word "believe" means more than mental assent or acknowledgement. It is not a detached stoicism. Rather, to believe is an act of faith and trust that Jesus is all that he claimed he was, and to turn one's life over to him in submission and obedience. To believe is to put the full weight of your hope and trust in him, not in yourself or anyone else. Verse 13 makes clear that it is through trusting in Christ alone that a person is saved. It is not based on genealogical heritage, which was the prevailing Jewish thought. The real children of God are born of faith, not of blood relationship.

The Jewish people believed they were God's beloved people by virtue of being descendants of Abraham. They believed this so strongly that when Jesus came as the true Messiah, they couldn't accept him. His teachings about the need to trust in him offended them, especially when Jesus said he was greater than Moses or Abraham and equated himself with God. Jesus didn't match their preconceived notions of a Messiah, so they rejected him.

Unfortunately, many people today suffer from the same disbelief. Some hold so tightly to their religious upbringing and family history that they think those things are enough to merit their salvation. Others cannot reconcile their preconceived ideas about Jesus with the reality of who he is, so they reject him based on their own ideas about him.

God Wrapped in Human Flesh (1:14–18)

Verse 14 is perhaps one of the most famous in the entire book of John because it summarizes the miracle of the incarnation—that God, in the person of Jesus Christ, wrapped himself in human skin and confined himself inside a frail, human body. God made his home among us, pitched his tent with us, and moved into our neighborhood. Fully divine and fully human, Jesus became both visible and tangible. He became one of us in order to redeem us out of our sinful state. It is a mystery that can never be fully explained.

Because Jesus' incarnation is such a mystery, human beings have tried to explain away one aspect of his being in favor of another. For instance, people called Gnostics believe that Jesus was not really human because human flesh was sinful. Muslims today believe that Jesus was not God incarnate, but rather a servant and messenger from God. Jews equate the worship of Jesus as God to idolatry. Obviously, what one believes about Jesus will shape one's entire belief system.

In verse 15, the gospel writer circled back to the testimony of John the Baptist to confirm Jesus' divinity and humanity. Without fully understanding the implications of his words, John proclaimed that Jesus was greater than he was because Jesus existed before him. Those who knew John and his family history would have known that he and Jesus were cousins, and that he (John) had been physically born *before* Jesus. The only way Jesus could have existed before John would be in his pre-incarnational state as the invisible God.

The mystery of the incarnation will never fully be understood this side of heaven. However, such limited knowledge should not keep us from believing its reality. Believing in something you cannot completely understand is not so difficult—it happens all the time. I cannot explain nor understand astrophysics, but I can still affirm its reality. I can't explain how gasoline makes an engine run (and I certainly can't explain the inner workings of that engine), but I drive my car almost daily.

Verses 16–17 reiterate the introduction of grace through the incarnation of Christ. Christ was "full of grace and truth" (1:14) and "grace and truth came through Jesus Christ" (1:17). Moses brought the Law. Jesus embodied grace and truth that would not only fulfill the law but would also make the law no longer necessary in order for someone to enjoy a relationship with God. Through Jesus' sacrificial death and resurrection, the sacrificial system in the Old Testament Law would no longer be needed.

Verse 18 closes out this ancient prologue by reminding readers that no one has seen God—not even Moses himself (1:17). Moses could see only a portion of God (Exodus

33:23), lest he die. Yet, in Jesus, the fullness of God is revealed. To know Jesus is to know God. While on earth, Jesus fully embodied the character of God.

Implications and Actions

Recognizing Jesus as God in the flesh, the only One in whom you can trust for salvation, is the most critical decision you will ever make. To believe in him as the Son of God who takes away the sins of the world will change not only your eternal destiny (heaven or hell), but it will also change the trajectory of your life every day. His Spirit will live within you, transforming you into his character as you surrender to him. You will discover that life is indeed found in him alone. The question is whether you will choose to trust in Jesus or if you will try to find life apart from him.

The Tent of Meeting (The Tabernacle)

When the gospel writer John described Jesus as God who "made his dwelling among us," he was using a term that would have been readily understood by the Jewish people. It was an allusion to the Tent of Meeting or Tabernacle depicted in the Book of Exodus. The Tent of Meeting was a portable place for the divine presence of

LESSON 1: *In Him Was Life*   35

God to dwell with his people (Israel) during their exodus from Egypt through the conquering of the land of Canaan. During the exodus and the years in exile, God's presence was indicated by a pillar of cloud covering the tent's entrance (Exodus 33:9). Moses often met with God there, as well as others who would inquire of the Lord. It was a place where God would reveal himself to his people. Once the Israelites took up residence in the Promised Land and constructed a permanent tabernacle, God met his people there. When God came to earth in the person of Jesus Christ, he was dwelling with his people—not in a place, but in a person.

APPLY THE TRUTH:

To apply the truths of this passage:

- Meditate on ways Jesus' character reflects the character of God.
- Notice how current culture tries to find life outside of Jesus.
- Thank God for the gift of being called a child of God because you believe in Jesus.

- Ask God to show you how to testify to others that Jesus is the light that will pierce the darkness in their lives.
- Watch for ways that Jesus reveals himself to you this week through the third person of the Trinity, the Holy Spirit, who resides in you as a believer.

QUESTIONS

1. How have you tried to wrap your mind around the concept of the Trinity, which is alluded to in these opening verses of John? How can God and Jesus be equal, yet different?

2. How have you seen people reject the light of Christ in their lives?

LESSON 1: *In Him Was Life* 37

3. Just like John the Baptist, believers today are called to tell others about Jesus. What obstacles do you face in doing this?

4. How do you feel knowing that God became flesh and dwelled among humanity? Why?

5. How did Jesus demonstrate both grace and truth? Which one do you lean towards as you relate to others?

6. What mysteries of the Christian faith do you accept and trust, even though you cannot understand them?

NOTES

1. Unless otherwise indicated, all Scripture quotations in lessons 1–6, 10–12, and the Christmas lesson are from the New International Version (1984 edition).

FOCAL TEXT
John 3:1–21

BACKGROUND
John 3:1–21

LESSON TWO
You Must Be Born Again

MAIN IDEA

The reward of eternal life requires a spiritual rebirth.

QUESTION TO EXPLORE

What does it mean to be born again?

STUDY AIM

To define what it means to be born again and to claim eternal life through Jesus Christ

QUICK READ

Many people believe you can get to heaven however you choose. John makes it clear that eternal life comes only by a spiritual rebirth through faith in Christ.

Introduction

"What happens after I die?" That one question summarizes the universal curiosity of people who want to know what occurs beyond this life. Will I go to heaven? Is there a hell? Do I just cease to exist? Knowing where we've come from and where we are going are among life's most important questions. In today's passage, Jesus provided the answer.

JOHN 3:1–21

1 Now there was a man of the Pharisees named Nicodemus, a member of the Jewish ruling council. **2** He came to Jesus at night and said, "Rabbi, we know you are a teacher who has come from God. For no one could perform the miraculous signs you are doing if God were not with him."

3 In reply Jesus declared, "I tell you the truth, no one can see the kingdom of God unless he is born again."

4 "How can a man be born when he is old?" Nicodemus asked. "Surely he cannot enter a second time into his mother's womb to be born!"

5 Jesus answered, "I tell you the truth, no one can enter the kingdom of God unless he is born of water and the Spirit. **6** Flesh gives birth to flesh, but the Spirit gives birth to spirit. **7** You should not be surprised at my saying,

'You must be born again.' **8** The wind blows wherever it pleases. You hear its sound, but you cannot tell where it comes from or where it is going. So it is with everyone born of the Spirit."

9 "How can this be?" Nicodemus asked.

10 "You are Israel's teacher," said Jesus, "and do you not understand these things? **11** I tell you the truth, we speak of what we know, and we testify to what we have seen, but still you people do not accept our testimony. **12** I have spoken to you of earthly things and you do not believe; how then will you believe if I speak of heavenly things? **13** No one has ever gone into heaven except the one who came from heaven—the Son of Man. **14** Just as Moses lifted up the snake in the desert, so the Son of Man must be lifted up, **15** that everyone who believes in him may have eternal life.

16 "For God so loved the world that he gave his one and only Son, that whoever believes in him shall not perish but have eternal life. **17** For God did not send his Son into the world to condemn the world, but to save the world through him. **18** Whoever believes in him is not condemned, but whoever does not believe stands condemned already because he has not believed in the name of God's one and only Son. **19** This is the verdict: Light has come into the world, but men loved darkness instead of light because their deeds were evil. **20** Everyone who does evil hates the light, and will not come into the light for fear that his deeds will be exposed. **21** But whoever lives by the truth comes into the light, so that it may be seen plainly that what he has done has been done through God."

Reborn in My Mother's Womb? (3:1–8)

This passage contains one of the most well-known verses in the Bible. It also introduces us to one of the most well-known characters in the New Testament—Nicodemus. Verse 1 provides some clues about this man. First, he was a Pharisee and a "member of the Jewish ruling council" (3:1). The Pharisees were a religious sect within Judaism who followed the whole law, written and oral. He was also on the ruling council, called the Sanhedrin, a political and religious group responsible for making sure the Law was upheld. They dealt with people who did not follow the laws regarding the temple, rituals, the Torah, tithes, and other matters.

In verse 2, Nicodemus called Jesus a rabbi and a teacher from God. This was a statement of respect and honor, especially since Nicodemus was an elite religious authority himself. He saw in Jesus something unique, something different from the religious men around him. Yet, he sought out Jesus at night, away from the crowds and under the cover of darkness. Perhaps this reflected Nicodemus' unwillingness to become identified as a follower of Jesus. It could have been incidental, since many conversations with rabbis took place at night. The night could even symbolize the state of Nicodemus' heart—in need of the Light of the world.

Jesus' statement in verse 3 must have completely leveled Nicodemus. First of all, Jesus did not thank Nicodemus for his flattering statements. Neither did he offer any observations about Nicodemus' goodness, which would have been a reciprocal response. After all Nicodemus was a devout Jew, a Pharisee, and even a member of the Sanhedrin. Jesus was in the presence of a popular and revered leader. Yet Jesus made no mention of this.

Secondly, Jesus skipped the formalities and jumped right into a deep theological discussion about the kingdom of God and those who could enter it. Likely Nicodemus thought he had already earned his spot in the kingdom of God because he was a Pharisee and a leader of his people. To talk about rebirth as the means of entrance into the kingdom would have been a radical departure from Nicodemus' understanding.

Nicodemus was obviously confused, because his conversation with Jesus centered on his efforts to grasp this concept. For Christians today, "born again" is a common term. It would have been radically new for Nicodemus. He did not understand that Jesus was referring to a spiritual rebirth through faith, rather than a second physical birth from the womb (3:4). While the prophets had spoken about spiritual rebirth (see Ezekiel 36:25-27; Jeremiah

31:31-34; Joel 2:28-32), Nicodemus' heart and mind had not made the connection.

Jesus' understanding of the location of the kingdom was also baffling to Nicodemus. The Jews were looking for an earthly Messiah who would overthrow Rome and establish an earthly kingdom. Jesus' mission was far different. He was concerned with a different kind of kingdom, the one where God Almighty reigned over both the heavens and the earth.

In the next few verses, Jesus continued to confound Nicodemus, dismantling his understanding of spiritual matters. Jesus explained that being born of water and spirit were both necessary for entrance into God's kingdom (John 3:5-6). Water referred to natural birth, and spirit referred to the Holy Spirit, the One who convicts the heart toward repentance.

Natural birth is accompanied by water (the breaking of the sac around a fetus); the Spirit brings spiritual rebirth, a rebirth that "must" happen (3:7). The term "must" is emphatic, leaving no other choice. Being reborn is the only means by which a person can enter the kingdom of God. This would have been a radical statement for a Jew to believe. Jews thought they were the rightful residents of God's kingdom because he had called them his chosen ones in the Old Testament.

In verses 8-9, Jesus used an element from nature as an illustration. A person can see the effects of the wind but not actually see the wind itself. In a similar manner a person can see the work of the Spirit through the changed lives he touches, even though one cannot see the Spirit. Jesus was explaining that Nicodemus did not necessarily need to understand everything about the rebirth in order for him to be reborn. The Spirit was at work in Nicodemus' life as well, even though he did not understand all that was going on.

I'm Still Confused (3:9–13)

Nicodemus still did not understand what Jesus was trying to tell him. He understood the Old Testament, but misunderstood what it said about Jesus as the Messiah (3:9). He taught the law but apparently did not connect the dots that led to Jesus.

When Jesus pointed out Nicodemus' lack of understanding (3:10), he was not trying to make fun of Nicodemus or chide him for his lack of insight. Rather, Jesus was trying to help Nicodemus understand that even the most learned scholars of Scripture (the Old Testament at that time) could completely miss out on the truth of the Messiah. For too many years, the Jewish people had approached their religious life from an earthly perspective, awaiting deliverance from the heavy-handed oppression of Rome. Because the Jewish people were so consumed with their life on earth, they could not look beyond their circumstances and believe in a Messiah who wrecked their expectations of his mission. They could not think of the kingdom as a heavenly one (3:12–13).

Many people today make the same mistake as the Jewish people did in Jesus' day. When God doesn't act according to our expectations, we are quick to dismiss him. We want him to meet our needs in this lifetime. While God cares about our daily lives he has a bigger picture in mind as he prepares us for eternity.

For God So Loved (3:14–18)

In verses 14–15, Jesus referred to an event that occurred in the Old Testament, recorded in Numbers 21:4–9. The people of Israel grumbled against God, so God sent venomous snakes that killed many of them. When Moses interceded, God commanded him to make a bronze snake and mount it on a pole that was raised above the people. Those who had been bitten could be saved from a poisonous death by looking at the uplifted bronze snake. Just as that bronze snake was lifted up to save the Israelites, Jesus was lifted up on a pole—the cross—so that those who look to him in faith can be saved from eternal death.

Verse 16 is undoubtedly the most famous Scripture in the Bible. Unfortunately, verses 17–18 often get overlooked because of the prominence of the previous verse. God did not send Jesus to condemn the world but to save it. To believe in him is to escape eternal condemnation;

LESSON 2: *You Must Be Born Again*   47

to refuse to believe ensures eternal damnation apart from the loving presence of God. God has made the provision for forgiveness and salvation, but every person must choose whether or not to believe in the "name of God's one and only Son" (3:18).

The Light of the World (3:19–21)

Jesus ended the conversation by pointing to himself as the Light. He had come into the world and had exposed sin and evil, but people preferred darkness to the light (3:19). Unfortunately, not much has changed in 2,000 years. Our world is full of people who prefer to live out their existence in darkness, evil, and sin rather than forsaking the darkness (3:20) and coming out into the light (3:21).

The story of Nicodemus doesn't end here. In John 19:39, the writer indicates that Nicodemus helped prepare Jesus' body for burial, which was a risky move, both politically and religiously. Had Nicodemus not believed in and followed Jesus, it is highly unlikely that he would have participated in Jesus' burial. At some point, Nicodemus' heart had been changed. We do not know when or where, but to take such a risk was evidence of his love for Jesus.

Nicodemus' story is also an illustration of how people come to Jesus in different ways. Nicodemus did not fall on his knees during this conversation and follow Jesus like others in the New Testament. Rather, his conversion was a quiet, unassuming one. The Bible does not record it with fanfare. His name was never mentioned in the "Roll Call of Faithful" in Hebrews 11. Still, his conversation with Jesus was recorded and serves as one of the most helpful sources to teach someone how to become a follower of Jesus. Like Nicodemus, we must all be born again by faith and trust in Jesus as Savior and Redeemer.

Applying This to Life

Jesus' assertion that you "must be born again" isn't very popular in today's culture. Some people prefer "buffet-style" spirituality that allows them to choose their beliefs from any number of religious or philosophical traditions. However, Jesus wasn't concerned about popularity. He spoke truth even when others disagreed, and the truth is that no one can go to heaven without repentance and trust in him as Savior and Lord.

We need to ask ourselves: Have I been born again? Have I trusted in Christ for forgiveness and redemption from sin? Or am I trying to earn my way to heaven? Do I believe that heaven is real? Or do I think there is no life after death? Do I believe heaven is reserved for those who follow Christ, or have I bought into the lie that being good and doing the right thing is enough to get into heaven?

The answers to those questions will determine not only the direction of your life, but also your destination for eternity. Answer carefully.

The Religious Elite:

Several different groups within Judaism existed during the time of Jesus. Here are the three main sects:

Pharisees: This splinter of Judaism was comprised of common people who strictly adhered to both the written law (the Torah) and oral law (commentary on the Torah); especially concerning the Sabbath, rituals, food restrictions, and other traditions. The Pharisees also believed in life after death and looked forward to a political Messiah who would bring world peace.

Sadducees: This offshoot of Judaism was comprised of priests and aristocrats who wanted to maintain the priestly caste system within the religion. They followed only the written law (the Torah) and rejected the oral law. They did not believe in life after death because it was not mentioned in the Torah. They focused on the rituals related to the temple.

Essenes: This group splintered off from mainline Judaism out of their disgust for both the Pharisees and Sadducees, whom they believed corrupted the temple. They lived a monastic life in the desert, following strict dietary laws and choosing to be celibate.

Who Needs to be Born Again?

On a sheet of paper, list people with whom you hope to enjoy heaven. Circle the ones who do not know about the need to be born again. Commit to pray about sharing this news with them. Then go and tell them the truth about how a person can enjoy heaven after death. Tell someone about your commitment so he or she can pray for you and ask you about your experience afterward.

QUESTIONS:

1. When you hear the term "born again" what comes to mind? Do you think it is a popular term today? Explain.

2. What questions did you have when you were introduced to Christianity? How were those questions similar or different from Nicodemus'?

3. In your sphere of influence, who needs to know they can have eternal life through Jesus?

4. What scares you about sharing the story of Nicodemus with others? How do you think others would respond to the need to be born again?

FOCAL TEXT
John 6:25–51

BACKGROUND
John 6:1–70

LESSON THREE
The Bread of Life

MAIN IDEA

Jesus satisfies our deepest hungers.

QUESTION TO EXPLORE

Who or what do we seek to satisfy our deepest needs?

STUDY AIM

To identify who or what I seek to satisfy my deepest needs and to choose Jesus to satisfy my hungers

QUICK READ

The world offers thousands of ways to satisfy the deepest hunger of our hearts. Unfortunately, all of them leave us longing for more. Only Jesus can satisfy the hunger in our hearts.

Introduction

Most likely you've never heard of Prader-Willi Syndrome (PWS). It's a rare disease that is often marked by a curious symptom: insatiable hunger. Unlike most people, sufferers of PWS do not experience the sensation of being full. They can literally eat themselves to death.

While that may sound like a horrible disease, many people suffer a similar problem spiritually. They will try anything to satisfy their spiritual hunger—money, success, power, others' opinions, drugs, and even food. Just like someone with PWS, those with spiritual hunger often die without ever discovering the One who alone can satisfy the deepest longings of the human heart.

JOHN 6:25–51

25 When they found him on the other side of the lake, they asked him, "Rabbi, when did you get here?"

26 Jesus answered, "I tell you the truth, you are looking for me, not because you saw miraculous signs but because you ate the loaves and had your fill. **27** Do not work for food that spoils, but for food that endures to eternal life, which the Son of Man will give you. On him God the Father has placed his seal of approval."

28 Then they asked him, "What must we do to do the works God requires?"

LESSON 3: *The Bread of Life*

29 Jesus answered, "The work of God is this: to believe in the one he has sent."

30 So they asked him, "What miraculous sign then will you give that we may see it and believe you? What will you do? **31** Our forefathers ate the manna in the desert; as it is written: 'He gave them bread from heaven to eat.'"

32 Jesus said to them, "I tell you the truth, it is not Moses who has given you the bread from heaven, but it is my Father who gives you the true bread from heaven. **33** For the bread of God is he who comes down from heaven and gives life to the world."

34 "Sir," they said, "from now on give us this bread."

35 Then Jesus declared, "I am the bread of life. He who comes to me will never go hungry, and he who believes in me will never be thirsty. **36** But as I told you, you have seen me and still you do not believe. **37** All that the Father gives me will come to me, and whoever comes to me I will never drive away. **38** For I have come down from heaven not to do my will but to do the will of him who sent me. **39** And this is the will of him who sent me, that I shall lose none of all that he has given me, but raise them up at the last day. **40** For my Father's will is that everyone who looks to the Son and believes in him shall have eternal life, and I will raise him up at the last day."

41 At this the Jews began to grumble about him because he said, "I am the bread that came down from heaven." **42** They said, "Is this not Jesus, the son of Joseph, whose father and mother we know? How can he now say, 'I came down from heaven'?"

43 "Stop grumbling among yourselves," Jesus answered. **44** "No one can come to me unless the Father who sent me draws him, and I will raise him up at the last day. **45** It is written in the Prophets: 'They will all be taught by God.' Everyone who listens to the Father and learns from him comes to me. **46** No one has seen the Father except the one who is from God; only he has seen the Father. **47** I tell you the truth, he who believes has everlasting life. **48** I am the bread of life. **49** Your forefathers ate the manna in the desert, yet they died. **50** But here is the bread that comes down from heaven, which a man may eat and not die. **51** I am the living bread that came down from heaven. If anyone eats of this bread, he will live forever. This bread is my flesh, which I will give for the life of the world."

Looking for a Sign (6:25–34)

Looking back at the preceding verses will set this story in context. Earlier in this chapter, Jesus performed two miracles: the feeding of the 5,000 (6:1–15) and walking on water (6:16–21). Because of his miracles, crowds followed after Jesus like a flock of crazed fans at a concert. In verse 26, Jesus challenged the fickle fanaticism of the crowd by pointing out their real motives for shadowing him. They sought him out because he had filled their stomachs with

LESSON 3: *The Bread of Life*

more bread and fish than they could eat—a rare treat in those days. They were not moved by empty hearts, but rather by empty stomachs. What else could this itinerate preacher give them?

In verses 27–29, Jesus spoke enigmatically to them, encouraging them to find the food that offers eternal life. He was not alluding to a works-based salvation. Rather, he was challenging the people to seek after eternal food—himself. Because he was cryptic in the way he talked to them, the people thought he was telling them that they could do something special to earn this eternal food. This prompted their questions in verse 28 and his response in verse 29. The people were focused on their actions—the "works of God" that could be exchanged for eternal life. Jesus was focused on their faith in him—"believe in the one he has sent" (6:29).

The response of the people is similar to the way people approach eternal life today. There are those who think they can perform enough good works to earn their way to eternal life. Help an elderly neighbor. Good. Teach a Sunday School class. Even better. Teach a bunch of first graders in VBS. Extra credit! But that merit system doesn't work because no amount of work can wipe away the sin in your life. Only through believing trust in Jesus can one obtain eternal life. It is a gift, not a paycheck that is earned through effort.

In verse 30, the people asked Jesus an audacious question: What sign will you do to prove you're from God?

This same group of people had just seen him perform two miracles, and yet, they wanted him to prove again that he was special, that he was who he claimed to be. Their skepticism and need for further proof is highlighted by their statement in verse 31. Their ancestors had eaten the manna that Moses had provided.

Why would the people use *that* story from Israelite history? Sure, Jesus could feed 5,000 people. But the real evidence of his authority as Messiah would come if he could work a greater miracle than Moses, who fed millions of men, women, and children. Only the Messiah sent from God could trump the work of their beloved ancestor Moses.

Jesus was quick to correct their understanding of history, and their theology, by pointing out the mistakes in their thinking. First, Moses had not provided the manna. God had (Exodus 16:4). Second, manna was not the real bread, meaning it was not the bread that would forever fulfill and sustain and give life (6:33). Only God alone could provide the real, lasting, eternal nourishment for the soul. That nourishment could only come from a person, not a loaf of bread or a mysterious food (manna) that appeared every morning. Third, this bread gives life "to the world" (6:33b). The Jews believed that only they, as the chosen people of God, could enjoy a relationship with God. However, Jesus came for all—both the religious and the pagan. Everyone has access to him.

Obviously, Jesus was pointing to himself as the "true bread" (6:32); but the people's hearts were still clouded, and they wanted Jesus to give them some bread that would meet their physical needs forever. Jesus was trying to move them beyond thinking about a full stomach to recognizing their empty hearts. But they missed it.

From our perspective, it's easy to judge the people for their dense thinking and their obsession with having their physical needs met. However, most of us are a lot like those people. How often do we look for God to meet our immediate needs without understanding that he is far more concerned about our spiritual and eternal needs? How often are our prayers focused on our immediate comfort? How often do we pray that God would do whatever it takes to draw us closer to him, even if that means we would suffer physically?

I Am What You're Looking For (6:35-40)

Jesus' words must have stunned his audience. In calling himself the Bread of Life, Jesus was not only calling himself superior to Moses, but also equal with Yahweh God. He was claiming to satisfy their deepest hunger and to squelch their deepest thirst. How could he make such an astonishing claim? Because he was God incarnate (John 1:14). He could meet their deepest longing because their deepest need was a saving relationship with him. He wanted their confidence to be rooted in him, not in signs or healings. He even laid out several reasons why the people could trust him:

He perfectly satisfies one's spiritual hunger (6:35b). Obviously, Jesus wasn't referring to physical hunger or thirst. Even Jesus experienced thirst and hunger. Rather, Jesus was claiming to be the One who could fully and completely satisfy.

1. He doesn't leave anyone out. Everyone is welcome to come to him (6:37). This must have been encouraging news to people who had been shunned by the religious community. He demonstrated this openness in his treatment of the marginalized—tax collectors, harlots, women, children, and sinners.

2. He doesn't have his own secret agenda for his desires (6:38). He wasn't trying to win a popularity contest. He wasn't chasing the applause of his peers. His sole desire was to follow God's plan for humanity, even though that plan hinged on Jesus' hanging on a cross.

3. He doesn't abandon those who come to him. They are safely held in his hands (6:39). Eternal life is guaranteed for those who believe in Jesus. What a comforting thought. This must have sounded too good to be true to a people who had not heard from a

LESSON 3: *The Bread of Life*

prophet in 400 years. To be reassured in this manner must have been like rain falling after a drought.

4. His pronouncement in these verses was radical to those within earshot. No one in the Jewish community—not even the High Priests or the religious elite—claimed such intimacy with God or such authority from God. No one claimed equality with God. It was considered blasphemy. Yet, Jesus did not shy away from the truth. He didn't care about appeasing the crowds or making people feel comfortable. His mission was to draw people to himself.

Not What We Were Expecting (6:41–51)

Like many of his other statements, Jesus' claim to be "the bread of life" caused quite an uproar among the people, especially the pious Jews and religious elite like the Pharisees. This man, this son of Joseph and Mary, could not have come from God. How could this child born to a teenage mother and a carpenter father possibly be God's Chosen One, the Messiah? No doubt, these questions must have swirled around in their heads. How could Jesus have come down from heaven if he'd been born as a baby just like everyone else? They never considered the fact that their preconceived notions about the Messiah could be wrong. They judged Jesus based on what they *thought* they knew about him, not the *truth* about him.

In much the same way, we may encounter people today who make judgments about Christianity based on what they *think* they know about Jesus. Without considering the possibility that their preconceived notions could be wrong, some think that Jesus is nothing more than a man who lived a good life, a prophet of God, or even an incarnation of Buddha. Those people who mistake the character and nature of Christ can miss out on a relationship with him.

In verse 43, Jesus confronted their grumbling by pointing back to his relationship with the Father. While the people claimed that Jesus didn't really know God, it was the people who really didn't understand God or his plan. The people could not accept the fact that Jesus— a traveling preacher, the son of a carpenter, with little money, no place to call home, and no religious backing—could be God in the flesh. Yahweh in their midst. They could not accept by faith the truth that to encounter Jesus is to encounter God the Father.

Jesus shifted the discussion back to his main point: he is the bread of life, and those who put their trust in him will never die (spiritually) (6:47–51). And like any good preacher, he used ordinary elements to communicate spiritual truths. This time, he spoke of his followers eating his body and his blood. In no way was Jesus legitimizing cannibalism. He was merely making a point: take

LESSON 3: *The Bread of Life*

me into your life and I will meet your deepest need. Drink of me—allow me to fill you up—and you will find satisfaction. Other pursuits will leave you empty and longing for more.

Implications and Actions

Jesus constantly drew people to himself. This story is just such an example. The same invitation to come to him for nourishment and life is still open to you and me today. The only way to satisfy the deepest longing in our souls is by trusting in the One who created those souls. The only way to find wholeness is by giving ourselves to the One who can make us whole. The only one who can truly give us eternal life is the One who died for us to make redemption possible. Seeking after anything else leaves us empty, longing, and searching.

MANNA

In the Old Testament, manna is described as "thin flakes like frost on the ground" (Exodus 16:13). It was white and tasted like wafers with honey (16:31). When the Israelites saw it, they asked "What is it?" (16:15), which is *man hu* in Hebrew. This is how the mysterious substance got its name (16:31).

Aside from feeding the Israelite people, the gathering of the manna was an act of faith. The people gathered only as much as they needed for each day and did not keep any extra for the next morning (16:19) as a symbol of their trust in God to provide for them. The only exception was on the sixth day of the week, when they were allowed to gather enough for the next day as well, the Sabbath (16:22–23).

God commanded that two quarts of manna be preserved throughout the generations as a reminder of how God fed the people in the wilderness (16:32). The Israelites ate the manna for forty years, until they reached the border of the land of Canaan, the land flowing with milk and honey (Exod. 33:3).

Applying this Scripture

- On a piece of paper, list things in your life that you use to try to ease your spiritual hunger. Spend time in prayer asking God to fill you.

- If something is creeping into your life and crowding out your time with God, fast from it as a commitment to find your joy and satisfaction in him alone.

- Ask God to show you any attempts to earn his favor by doing good deeds.

LESSON 3: *The Bread of Life*

- Pay attention to social media, TV shows, movies, and other influences that tempt you to seek fulfillment in places other than God.

- Memorize John 6:35 as a weapon against the temptation to find satisfaction in things other than God.

QUESTIONS

1. What reasons do people give today for choosing not to come to Jesus for their spiritual nourishment and fulfillment?

2. In what ways is following Jesus different from what you were expecting?

3. When have you been guilty of wanting a sign or miracle from God as proof of his presence or his watchcare over you?

4. Talk about a time when you felt deep physical hunger. How does that experience compare to a time when you deeply hungered for God?

5. Talk about a time in your past when you tried to fill your spiritual hunger with something other than God. What was the result?

FOCAL TEXT
John 8:31–47

BACKGROUND
John 8:12–59

LESSON FOUR
The Truth Will Set You Free

MAIN IDEA

Through Jesus (truth personified) we are freed from sin and free to follow God.

QUESTION TO EXPLORE

What does it mean to be truly free?

STUDY AIM

To discover the biblical definition of freedom and to choose a life of true freedom

QUICK READ

In this conversation with the Jewish people, whose ancestors had been slaves in Egypt, Jesus proclaimed that as the Son of God, only he could truly set them free.

Introduction

In today's worldwide political landscape, the desire to exercise freedom is the source of many conflicts, uprisings, and even outright war. Regimes are toppling, citizens are demanding choices in the leadership of their country, and many people are giving their lives in order to ensure freedom for future generations. While the exercise of freedom is a human right, many people are enslaved and don't even know it. They are held captive to sin and death, but assume that because they can do anything they want, they are free. Today's lesson is a reminder that true freedom can only come through a relationship with Jesus Christ.

JOHN 8:31–47

31 To the Jews who had believed him, Jesus said, "If you hold to my teaching, you are really my disciples. **32** Then you will know the truth, and the truth will set you free."

33 They answered him, "We are Abraham's descendants and have never been slaves of anyone. How can you say that we shall be set free?"

34 Jesus replied, "I tell you the truth, everyone who sins is a slave to sin. **35** Now a slave has no permanent place in the family, but a son belongs to it forever. **36** So if the

Son sets you free, you will be free indeed. **37** I know you are Abraham's descendants. Yet you are ready to kill me, because you have no room for my word. **38** I am telling you what I have seen in the Father's presence, and you do what you have heard from your father."

39 "Abraham is our father," they answered.

"If you were Abraham's children," said Jesus, "then you would do the things Abraham did. **40** As it is, you are determined to kill me, a man who has told you the truth that I heard from God. Abraham did not do such things. **41** You are doing the things your own father does."

"We are not illegitimate children," they protested. "The only Father we have is God himself."

42 Jesus said to them, "If God were your Father, you would love me, for I came from God and now am here. I have not come on my own; but he sent me. **43** Why is my language not clear to you? Because you are unable to hear what I say. **44** You belong to your father, the devil, and you want to carry out your father's desire. He was a murderer from the beginning, not holding to the truth, for there is no truth in him. When he lies, he speaks his native language, for he is a liar and the father of lies. **45** Yet because I tell the truth, you do not believe me! **46** Can any of you prove me guilty of sin? If I am telling the truth, why don't you believe me? **47** He who belongs to God hears what God says. The reason you do not hear is that you do not belong to God."

What Real Freedom Looks Like (8:31–36)

This story took place during the Feast of Tabernacles, one of the required pilgrimages to Jerusalem so that the Jewish people could present their offerings and worship Yahweh. Families from every corner of the country had come to fulfill their religious duty. It was against this religious backdrop that Jesus spoke, and many people believed in him (8:30).

Today's passage begins with Jesus telling the believing Jews they needed to "hold to my teaching" (8:31). These Jews had agreed with Jesus' teaching; but only by *following* and *acting* on his words would they show what they truly believed about him. By following Jesus' words, they would know the truth and would be set free by it (8:32). By following Jesus, they would come to understand that everything Jesus had said (and would say) was the foundational truth upon which to build their lives. They would understand him as the way, the truth, and the life (John 14:6).

Jesus was saying that true belief is more than stating what you believe, but rather reveals itself in the life and actions of the one who believes. In this instance, the faith of these Jews was fickle, because by the end of this chapter, they were ready to stone Jesus (8:59). Apparently, they had not believed in his words as truth coming from God.

In verse 33, the people became indignant and proud, resting on their belief that as descendants of Abraham

(Genesis 12:2), they were God's chosen people. How dare this young preacher from the backwoods of Nazareth accuse them of being enslaved by anyone? Sadly, the Jews had forgotten their heritage. Centuries before, the Israelites had been enslaved for 400 years at the hands of the Egyptians. Not to mention all of the times the people of God had been taken captive by foreign armies and forced to live as scattered people away from their homeland. The Israelites had known slavery, even slavery to idols. The Old Testament chronicles the repeated idolatry of the children of Israel. They had bowed to idols and had been enslaved by pagan cultures.

It might be easy to judge the Jews for their forgetfulness of their own sinfulness. However, one look in the mirror or one glance back at our own history should be a reminder of how easily believers can forget their sinful behavior, only to repeat it again. When the grace and mercy of God becomes a distant memory instead of a daily focus, arrogance and pride can creep in and take root. We can become blinded to our own penchant to applaud ourselves for our "grand spirituality"—much like the Jews in this story.

Understanding the heart and mindset of the crowd, Jesus made it clear that sin enslaves everyone (8:34), no matter their religious heritage. The only way to experience true freedom is through the Son. Jesus was foreshadowing his death and resurrection that would purchase the pardon that would open the doors of the prison of sin.

These must have been hard words for the Jews to accept. They had relied on their own merits to find favor with God. But those same words found receptive ears from the people who were painfully aware of their own sinfulness. Only the grace of God could set them free.

Following God the Father (8:37–42)

Rather than applaud the descendants of Abraham for their fine upbringing and outstanding pedigree, Jesus cut to the heart of the matter, undoubtedly infuriating them in the process. Jesus denounced the Jews for rejecting his words as one who spoke for God the Father. In essence, Jesus was equating himself with God, the most heinous of sins in the Israelites' eyes. This was considered blasphemy, a charge that would be brought against him at his trial (John 19:7) He declared that *he* was God's anointed, that God was *his* Father, and that the Jews had a different father altogether (8:38).

Basically, Jesus was calling the Jews a bunch of illegitimate children (a derisive term usually reserved for the much-maligned Samaritan half-breeds). At this point, the Israelites were beyond furious, dumbfounded at such accusations and slander. No one had ever spoken to the Jews with such irreverence and lack of respect. No one had ever called out the Jewish leaders and challenged their relationship with God. Certainly no one had ever

LESSON 4: *The Truth Will Set You Free* 75

denied that the Jews were the people of God. Yet, in this one encounter, Jesus completely shattered their paradigm and ushered in a new way of thinking and believing in God.

The people within earshot would have plenty to tell their friends and family at the supper table. It would be the stuff of Facebook posts and Twitter feeds today. Predictably, the Jews objected to Jesus' declaration, reminding Jesus that Abraham was their father (8:39). They were still blinded by their title as God's chosen, and misunderstood the foundation of a relationship with God.

When Jesus talked about the Israelites' father, he was not referring to biological lineage but rather the lineage of faith. He set forth new criteria for fellowship with God, a relationship not based on *genealogy* but on *grace*. This concept was simply untenable to the Jewish leaders. Grace had been forgotten long ago and had been replaced by a system built on laws upon laws, rituals, and outward displays of spiritual superiority. Relationship, real relationship, the kind of relationship that Abraham had with God, had been replaced by religious duty. No relationship can survive on duty. Before long the relationship will be nothing more than a hollow shell of what could have been.

People today can suffer from the same lack of faith. They may mistakenly believe their biological lineage can save them. They may attempt to rely on the faith of their parents and go through the motions of religious activity—just like the Jews did—and believe those actions are what God desires. Jesus was breathing fresh wind into the sails of faith which the people of God had lived by for centuries.

The "Roll Call of the Faithful" in Hebrews 11 contains the names of some of those persons who had lived by faith even before the coming of the Messiah. Gideon. Barak. Abraham. Moses. All of them lived by faith and not by sight, looking ahead to a time when the Redeemer would make all things new. Unfortunately, the Jews could not let go of their preconceived notions of the Messiah and rejected Jesus as the Chosen One who would bring freedom to the captives (Isaiah 61:1). Jesus can be rejected because of similar reasons today. Some people cannot let go of their expectations and assumptions about Jesus, and in doing so, become enslaved by their own ideology.

Following the Father of Lies (8:43–47)

The exchange between Jesus and the Jewish people escalated in these last few verses. Jesus left no room for misinterpretation. He accused the Jewish leaders of having the devil as their father, which was an insult beyond all others. The tension in that moment must have been palpable. How dare this nobody, this carpenter from Nazareth call God's chosen people children of the devil. This statement completely alienated the Jews. And yet, Jesus did not back away. He did not try to make nice or

LESSON 4: *The Truth Will Set You Free*

compromise. He would speak the truth because that is his very nature (8:45; 14:6).

The Jews refused to listen to the Truth Giver (Jesus) and instead chose to believe the lies of the devil, who has no truth in him. They had been listening to the lies of Satan for so long they could no longer recognize the truth. Their lack of faith and refusal to believe in Jesus revealed their true character. Their behavior would mirror their beliefs. In some ways, Jesus was predicting what would take place later in his ministry. The Jews would completely reject Jesus and incite his death. They indeed followed the actions of the devil, the one who had been a murderer from the beginning (8:44).

Jesus made it clear. Those who belong to God listen to and heed his words (8:47). To reject Jesus' teachings is to reject God because the two are one and the same. This assertion rubs against the grain of today's modern culture, which encourages people to choose what they will believe and obey, and leave the rest untouched, as if Christianity were a buffet. You cannot decide to follow Jesus in part. He requires full surrender and unqualified obedience. That is the essence of the life of faith. Everything else leads to spiritual slavery.

Life Application

Jesus' call to experience him as truth that can set the captive free still stands true for us today. We can choose to listen to him, or we can listen to the father of lies who wants nothing more than to kill, steal, and destroy us (John 10:10). The devil's lies are abundant—one of which is the lie that sin does not lead to slavery and death. Many people are blind to their own enslavement to sin. Believing they are free, they do not see how sin controls their lives and leads them to destruction. We as believers must choose daily to submit ourselves to Christ, because only then can we truly experience the freedom that he provides.

NAMES FOR THE DEVIL IN SCRIPTURE

The Bible uses several words for the devil, all with unique and descriptive meanings that describe the many facets of his malevolent character. He is the embodiment of evil. Here are some of the most notable names in the Bible:

- **Accuser:** Means "to speak against." It is a legal term and refers to the accusations Satan levels against believers. (Revelation 12:10)
- **Abaddon:** Means "destroying angel" (Revelation 9:11)

LESSON 4: *The Truth Will Set You Free*

- **Adversary:** Means "opponent" or "enemy" (1 Peter 5:8)
- **Belial:** Means "worthlessness" or "wicked" (2 Corinthians 6:15)
- **Tempter:** Refers to Satan's attempts to entice people to sin (Matthew 4:3)
- **Beelzebub:** Literally means "lord of the house" and refers to the devil being the chief of the evil spirits (Luke 11:15)
- **Wicked One:** The word "wicked" is used in an ethical sense (Matthew. 13:38–39).
- **Lucifer:** Means "shining one" or "morning star" (Isaiah 14:12)
- **Satan:** Means "adversary" or "one who opposes" God and Jesus, and who incites people to turn from God and to sin (Mark 1:13).

Who Are You Listening To?

This week, assess how truth is presented in the media (TV, movies, music, social media, etc.) Evaluate whether or not the world's ideology is creeping into your relationship with the Lord. For example, does watching TV cause you to question God's word? Are you following the voice of truth or the voice of the enemy? Perhaps you need to take a break from certain types of media that tempt you to listen to the enemy rather than Christ.

QUESTIONS

1. Can you remember what your life was like before you knew Christ? How did sin enslave you?

2. What are some modern day idols that enslave people who worship them?

LESSON 4: *The Truth Will Set You Free*

3. What do you think happens to a person's faith development when he or she develops pride or arrogance about his or her spiritual heritage?

4. What lies from the father of lies have you been listening to? How can you counter these lies with God's truth?

5. How can you distinguish the voice of the Father from the voice of the devil?

FOCAL TEXT
John 10:1–21

BACKGROUND
John 9:35–10:21

LESSON FIVE
Life to the Full

MAIN IDEA

Jesus, the Good Shepherd, wants to lead us to a life full of purpose, peace, and joy.

QUESTION TO EXPLORE

How can we experience a life full of purpose, peace, and joy?

STUDY AIM

To recognize the voice of Jesus and to choose to accept his offer of a life full of purpose, peace, and joy

QUICK READ

Jesus called himself the Good Shepherd who would lead his followers into a life full of purpose, peace, and joy. He would eventually give his life for their well-being.

Introduction

A television documentary educated me about the changing nature of advertising in our culture. Advertisers used to try to sell products by persuading us about the performance of their brands. A certain detergent would get our clothes cleaner; a certain deodorant would keep us drier; and a certain toilet paper was more squeezable.

Now, though, advertisers go beyond simple performance in the promotion of their products. They employ what is called "emotional branding." This technique promises a certain quality of life in return for using their product. They promise that their brand will add meaning to your life and make your life more joyful and abundant. Their brand will fill the empty places in your life, and if you do not own their brand your life will be empty and incomplete.

Everyone wants to have a life that is full of purpose, peace, and joy. Jesus challenges the prevailing cultural solutions that promise to produce that kind of life. Jesus insisted that a truly abundant life comes by following him.

JOHN 10:1–21

1 "I tell you the truth, the man who does not enter the sheep pen by the gate, but climbs in by some other way, is a thief and a robber. **2** The man who enters by the gate

LESSON 5: *Life to the Full*

is the shepherd of his sheep. **3** The watchman opens the gate for him, and the sheep listen to his voice. He calls his own sheep by name and leads them out. **4** When he has brought out all his own, he goes on ahead of them, and his sheep follow him because they know his voice. **5** But they will never follow a stranger; in fact, they will run away from him because they do not recognize a stranger's voice." **6** Jesus used this figure of speech, but they did not understand what he was telling them.

7 Therefore Jesus said again, "I tell you the truth, I am the gate for the sheep. **8** All who ever came before me were thieves and robbers, but the sheep did not listen to them. **9** I am the gate; whoever enters through me will be saved. He will come in and go out, and find pasture. **10** The thief comes only to steal and kill and destroy; I have come that they may have life, and have it to the full.

11 "I am the good shepherd. The good shepherd lays down his life for the sheep. **12** The hired hand is not the shepherd who owns the sheep. So when he sees the wolf coming, he abandons the sheep and runs away. Then the wolf attacks the flock and scatters it. **13** The man runs away because he is a hired hand and cares nothing for the sheep.

14 "I am the good shepherd; I know my sheep and my sheep know me— **15** just as the Father knows me and I know the Father—and I lay down my life for the sheep. **16** I have other sheep that are not of this sheep pen. I must bring them also. They too will listen to my voice, and there shall be one flock and one shepherd. **17** The reason my Father loves me is that I lay down my life—only to take it up again. **18** No one takes it from me, but I lay it down of my own accord. I have authority to lay it down and authority to take it up again. This command I received from my Father."

19 At these words the Jews were again divided. **20** Many of them said, "He is demon-possessed and raving mad. Why listen to him?"

21 But others said, "These are not the sayings of a man possessed by a demon. Can a demon open the eyes of the blind?"

Follow the Shepherd (10:1–6)

Jesus used an analogy to challenge the prevailing opinion of the Pharisees about what it meant to have a full life. The meaning of the analogy seemed to have eluded the Pharisees, at least at first. Perhaps they could not see themselves in the words Jesus spoke.

The analogy came from the world of shepherds and sheep. Our experience with the world of sheep may be more limited. It was a familiar subject where Jesus lived and the Pharisees should have understood what Jesus was talking about. After all, shepherds and sheep were images often used in the Old Testament Scriptures to describe God's relationship with Israel.

LESSON 5: *Life to the Full* 87

In the ancient Middle East, shepherds often brought their sheep to a community sheep pen at night. The flocks of different shepherds would be housed in the same pen where they would be safe from wild animals that might attack in the dark. The shepherds would leave the sheep with a watchman during the night. In the morning the shepherd would return, be admitted entrance by the watchman through the gate, and call out for his sheep to follow him. The sheep recognized the voice of their particular shepherd and would separate themselves from the rest of the flocks in the pen and follow their shepherd back out into the fields. The sheep that belonged to a shepherd recognized his disctinctive voice and would not follow any other person.

Sheep trust their shepherd and will follow him through the gate of the pen into the abundance that awaits them. Jesus used this analogy to illustrate how his followers hear his voice and trust him to provide a life that is full and abundant. Jesus has called us out and we must trust him enough to follow him.

Beware of Thieves and Robbers! (10:7–10)

Jesus is our shepherd, but he also compared himself to the gate of the sheep pen. The only valid path to an abundant life is through the gate. Jesus warned that there are some who would try to take us another way. Jesus reminded his followers of voices who would attempt to "pull the wool over their eyes" (pun intended) about what it means to have a full and abundant life. Jesus understood that we have a tendency to fall prey to false promises from the wolves of the world.

In the immediate context, Jesus may have been referring to the Pharisees, who in the ninth chapter of John had just thrown a man out of the synagogue for having the audacity to be healed of blindness on the Sabbath Day. Their insistence on enforcing a strict interpretation of the Sabbath laws had the effect of robbing him of an abundant life. Jesus described the Pharisees as robbers and thieves. They were not interested in the well-being of the man. Their interest was in promoting themselves and their agenda.

Spiritual thieves and robbers are still present and seek to carry people away. Maybe it is the health and wealth preacher on television with slick hair and a big smile who is fleecing the flock for personal profit. Perhaps we get carried away by the robber barons of Wall Street or Madison Avenue who try to convince us that abundant life comes from an abundance of possessions. Maybe we hear the voices of a political party which tries to convince us that their platform is God's way to a meaningful life. Voices are out there; voices are calling; voices whisper and shout and plead and beg, promising abundant life. But the truth is they are thieves and robbers who are not concerned about the sheep at all. They are concerned

LESSON 5: *Life to the Full*

with themselves and their own agendas, and we have fallen prey to them.

Thieves and robbers exist, Jesus said. They want to take you out over the wall instead of through the gate. They want to devour you. The only safe path is to follow the voice of the Shepherd as he leads us though the gate. The way to life, full life, is through Jesus.

The Good Shepherd Cares for His Sheep (10:11–18)

Jesus declared himself to be the "good shepherd." A good shepherd would give his life for the sheep. That, of course, is exactly what Jesus did a few weeks later when the Good Shepherd became the Lamb that was slain.

Jesus acknowledged the presence of bad shepherds. He likened them to hired hands who do not own the sheep, they simply tend them for the owner. Hired hands are in the business of shepherding for what it will provide them. They will not sacrifice themselves for the sheep because they have no sense of ownership. When danger comes they abandon their post in order to save themselves, leaving the sheep defenseless.

Remember, Jesus is not speaking these words out in green pastures or beside still waters. He is speaking in the context of conflict, surrounded by the Pharisees he is accusing of being bad shepherds. We may think Jesus was referring to Psalm 23 when he declared himself to be the good shepherd, but I rather think he was referring to Ezekiel 34 when he was directing these words at the Pharisees. Ezekiel 34 says,

> Woe to the shepherds of Israel who only take care of themselves! Should not shepherds take care of the flock? You eat the curds, clothe yourselves with the wool and slaughter the choice animals, but you do not take care of the flock. You have not strengthened the weak or healed the sick or bound up the injured. You have not brought back the strays or searched for the lost. You have ruled them harshly and brutally.
>
> EZEKIEL 34:1B–4

Jesus was accusing the Pharisees of being bad shepherds.

There are still bad shepherds in religious life. There are religious leaders who are guilty of spiritual abuse; who are more interested in personal gain than sacrifice for others. This may take the form of greed, craving for power, sexual gratification, or the need to bolster one's self-esteem. Some refuse to be accountable to anyone, while others try to control the thoughts and actions of people by instilling fear in the hearts of those they are called to lead. These spiritual leaders are bad shepherds and we should be aware of them.

LESSON 5: *Life to the Full*

The good news is that the Christian faith is not about bad shepherds. Our faith is in the Good Shepherd. The Good Shepherd knows us and loves us and laid down his life for us. Jesus also pointed out that no one took his life. He gave his life voluntarily because he knew it was necessary for the well-being of his sheep. He knew that in surrendering his life he could lead us into a life that was full and abundant.

Jesus did not give his life only for the lost sheep of Israel. He gave his life for the sake of the whole world. The Pharisees were convinced that God only wanted to save Israel but Jesus knew there were millions of lost sheep who were "not of this sheep pen" (John 10:16). He was referring to Gentiles who would also follow the Shepherd into an abundant life.

Thankfully God has given us ears to distinguish the voice of the Good Shepherd from the other voices that are calling us. Jesus' voice comes to us openly and honestly; not a voice that tries to confuse or deceive us. It is the voice of one who cares about us, not one who is selfishly seeking his own advancement. Jesus is the one who serves and sacrifices, not one who fleeces and fools.

Choosing a Life that is Full (10:19–21)

After Jesus' discourse, the Pharisees had a choice to make. Would they follow the Good Shepherd into a full life or would they continue to rob themselves and others of the life Jesus offered? We face the same decision.

Some thought Jesus was a madman, perhaps even demon-possessed. They obviously did not recognize the voice of the Good Shepherd.

Others, however, seemed to hear a whisper of hope. As they thought about what Jesus had said they began to recognize the voice of a shepherd who loved his sheep. They saw Jesus doing things only God could do. Some of them may have even gone through the gate to follow Jesus into a life that was full.

Implications and Actions

The key to a full and abundant life is found in following Jesus, the Good Shepherd. The Good Shepherd cares for us, unlike bad shepherds who care only for themselves. We do not usually associate an abundant life with being a follower. We often think of leaders as the people who live abundantly. But Jesus says that a full and abundant life comes when we follow him.

A young woman wanted to go off to college but her heart sank when she read the question on the application that asked, "Are you a leader?" Being both honest and conscientious she wrote, "No." She returned the application, expecting the worst. To her surprise she received a letter from the college: "Dear Applicant: A study of the application forms reveals that this year our college will have 1,452 new leaders. We are accepting you because we feel it is imperative that we have at least one follower."

Obviously, we do need leaders in this world. But remember that as Christians, we are primarily followers. We are followers of that unique, singular, recognizable voice that takes us to abundant places. They are not places necessarily filled with fancy cars and big houses and positions of power. Following Jesus is not about possessions; it is about *purpose*. Abundant life is not about purchasing the right product or electing the right politician or even about hearing the right preacher. Life that is full and abundant comes from following the right voice: the voice of the Good Shepherd.

Sheep and Shepherds

Jesus used a metaphor that was very familiar to his audience. The Old Testament was full of references to pastoral life when describing God's relationship with his people. A few examples:

Psalm 23:1—"The Lord is my Shepherd, I shall not be in want."

Psalm 78:52—"But he brought his people out like a flock; he led them like sheep through the desert."

Isaiah 40:11—"He tends his flock like a shepherd: He gathers the lambs in his arms."

An example of bad shepherds is found in Jeremiah 23:1-4, which begins: "Woe to the shepherds who are destroying and scattering the sheep of my pasture!"

The metaphor Jesus used was common and the Pharisees should have understood his words.

Rebuilding Trust

A woman is visiting your Sunday School class but seems very nervous. She shares with you that in her last church the leadership was very controlling. They told her that if she did not do everything they told her to do, she would be in disobedience to God. Some of the things she was told to do made her very uncomfortable, but she was afraid to disobey the leaders. Now she is nervous about church and does not trust any spiritual leader. How can you help her?

Questions

1. How can you distinguish between the voice of Jesus and the voices in our culture when making decisions?

LESSON 5: *Life to the Full* 95

2. Discuss the issue of spiritual abuse in religious life today. What are the characteristics of spiritual abuse? Why do some people fall prey to spiritual abusers? How can we help people who have been victims of spiritual abuse?

3. What are the characteristics of a good spiritual leader?

4. What does Jesus mean when he says that he has come to give life to the full? What does a full, abundant life look like?

5. Name some of the things in our culture that deceive us about what it means to have a full and abundant life. These may come from the realm of philosophy, marketing, politics, etc.

6. How could you experience more of the full and abundant life Jesus offers?

FOCAL TEXT
John 11:17–44

BACKGROUND
John 11:1–57

LESSON SIX
The Resurrection and the Life

MAIN IDEA

The raising of Lazarus revealed Jesus as the source of resurrection life.

QUESTION TO EXPLORE

How should I respond to Jesus as the source of resurrection life?

STUDY AIM

To define resurrection life and to experience this life by placing my faith and trust in Jesus

QUICK READ

The raising of Lazarus from the dead was a sign pointing to Jesus as the true source of life. Jesus is Lord, even over death.

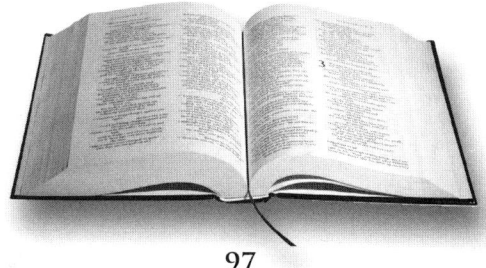

Introduction

I have been a pastor for twenty-seven years. During those years I have conducted hundreds of funerals. I have stood at equally numerous gravesides with weeping family members who gathered in grief before their loved one would be lowered into the ground. It is never a happy affair. From our point of view, death is the final insult, an enemy too powerful to overcome. It is the end of relationships, the end of dreams, and the end of hope. Our family members and friends are not going to get better.

In all of the years I have been presiding at funerals, I have never seen someone come back to life. There is a cemetery behind our church. I have never seen one of the graves burst open with a live person climbing out. It all seems so hopeless.

Believers in Jesus, though, know it is not hopeless. We have hope because we believe Jesus is not only Lord of life, but also Lord over death. When he raised his friend Lazarus from the dead he proved that what he told Martha was true. Even today when we stand at a graveside we find confident assurance and hope in the words of Jesus: "I am the resurrection and the life" (John 11:25).

LESSON 6: *The Resurrection and the Life*

JOHN 11:17–44

17 On his arrival, Jesus found that Lazarus had already been in the tomb for four days. **18** Bethany was less than two miles from Jerusalem, **19** and many Jews had come to Martha and Mary to comfort them in the loss of their brother. **20** When Martha heard that Jesus was coming, she went out to meet him, but Mary stayed at home.

21 "Lord," Martha said to Jesus, "if you had been here, my brother would not have died. **22** But I know that even now God will give you whatever you ask."

23 Jesus said to her, "Your brother will rise again."

24 Martha answered, "I know he will rise again in the resurrection at the last day."

25 Jesus said to her, "I am the resurrection and the life. He who believes in me will live, even though he dies; **26** and whoever lives and believes in me will never die. Do you believe this?"

27 "Yes, Lord," she told him, "I believe that you are the Christ, the Son of God, who was to come into the world."

28 And after she had said this, she went back and called her sister Mary aside. "The Teacher is here," she said, "and is asking for you." **29** When Mary heard this, she got up quickly and went to him. **30** Now Jesus had not yet entered the village, but was still at the place where Martha had met him. **31** When the Jews who had been with Mary in the house, comforting her, noticed how quickly she got up and went out, they followed her, supposing she was going to the tomb to mourn there.

32 When Mary reached the place where Jesus was and saw him, she fell at his feet and said, "Lord, if you had been here, my brother would not have died."

33 When Jesus saw her weeping, and the Jews who had come along with her also weeping, he was deeply moved in spirit and troubled. **34** "Where have you laid him?" he asked.

"Come and see, Lord," they replied.

35 Jesus wept.

36 Then the Jews said, "See how he loved him!"

37 But some of them said, "Could not he who opened the eyes of the blind man have kept this man from dying?" **38** Jesus, once more deeply moved, came to the tomb. It was a cave with a

stone laid across the entrance. **39** "Take away the stone," he said.

"But, Lord," said Martha, the sister of the dead man, "by this time there is a bad odor, for he has been there four days."

40 Then Jesus said, "Did I not tell you that if you believed, you would see the glory of God?" **41** So they took away the stone. Then Jesus looked up and said, "Father, I thank you that you have heard me. **42** I knew that you always hear me, but I said this for the benefit of the people standing here, that they may believe that you sent me."

LESSON 6: *The Resurrection and the Life* 101

43 When he had said this, Jesus called in a loud voice, "Lazarus, come out!" **44** The dead man came out, his hands and feet wrapped with strips of linen, and a cloth around his face.

Jesus said to them, "Take off the grave clothes and let him go."

Where Is Jesus When We Need Him? (11:1–16)

The background text sets the scene. Jesus received word his friend Lazarus was sick. Lazarus had two sisters, Mary and Martha. All three seem to have been special friends of Jesus. Mary and Martha sent word to Jesus that Lazarus was sick and presumably intended for Jesus to come running. They knew Jesus was a healer and his presence might prevent their worst fears from coming true.

But Jesus did not go, at least not at first. He was not there to heal Lazarus and he was not present when Lazarus died. He did not even go to the funeral! When he finally decided to go, he knew Lazarus was already dead. Everyone must have thought it was too late for Jesus to do any good. But Jesus knew his timing was right. He knew his delay would result in glory for God and would strengthen the faith of his disciples.

When Jesus Comes Too Late (11:17–32)

Jesus finally arrived, but it seemed to be too late. Lazarus had already been in the tomb four days. There was a common Jewish belief that the spirit of a person hovered around the body for three days before departing, so four days after death, all hope would have been lost. Lazarus was as dead as dead could be.

Martha went out to meet Jesus on the road. "Lord," she said. "If you had been here my brother would not have died" (11:21). At first glance this seems like a stinging rebuke borne from the frustration of Jesus' intentional delay. There must have been some anger mixed with her grief. On the other hand, it was also a statement of faith. Martha believed Jesus could have saved Lazarus when no one else could. She even stated her continued faith that God was still working through Jesus, even if she thought Jesus' arrival was too late.

Later, Mary expressed the very same words (11:32). Though she must have been frustrated with the absence of Jesus during the critical moments of Lazarus' illness, she also believed that Jesus could have healed him when everyone else had lost hope.

The sisters had faith in Jesus as the lord of life, but they had not yet come to realize that he was also lord over death. When Jesus told Martha that Lazarus would rise again she expressed a nebulous faith in the resurrection

LESSON 6: *The Resurrection and the Life*

on judgment day, but she could not fathom God's plan for that day.

Jesus interrupted her limited faith by announcing, "I AM the resurrection and the life" (11:25). Note he did not say "I will be the resurrection and the life," but "I AM." It is reminiscent of God's revelation of himself to Moses at the burning bush (Exodus 3). Jesus was not a savior only for the future, but for the present as well. He is lord over death, not just on the last day, but every day: even today!

Admittedly, God does not choose to raise people from the dead every day. Even when Jesus was walking on the earth he did not raise everyone who died. Soon he would raise Lazarus, but even Lazarus would die again. Jesus was declaring to Martha that he was Lord; not only of life, but also over death. Soon he would prove it again when he himself rose from the grave.

Jesus expanded on this thought by telling Martha that people who believe in him could expect life! Even if they died, death was not the end. In God's design, life goes on even after we die!

Jesus asked Martha if she believed him. Like us, she may not have understood everything about eternal life, but she did believe in Jesus. She believed that Jesus was the Christ, the Son of God. Like us, she may have found Jesus' words difficult to understand. But she trusted that Jesus knew what he was talking about. She believed Jesus.

All of us have had moments when we were frustrated that Jesus did not show up to save the day. When a loved one is sick and dying, when a marriage is dissolving, when the bankers are coming to foreclose, we expect Jesus to show up and save us. When the worst happens we assume it is too late. But Jesus knows what he is doing. We continue to believe in Jesus even when it is difficult to understand. For those who place their faith in Jesus, even death is not the final word.

Jesus Cares When We Hurt (11:33–37)

Jesus seemed to arrive too late but that did not mean that he did not care. He just had bigger things in mind. When we are hurting and Jesus is nowhere to be found, it does not mean he does not care. It just means his plans are bigger than we can see.

"Jesus wept," (11:35) the Bible says. It is the favorite verse of most boys and girls who are assigned to memorize a Bible verse. But have you ever stopped to think about why Jesus wept?

Some might be tempted to think Jesus wept because Lazarus was dead. After all, that is why Mary and Martha were weeping. That is why the Jews who had come to visit Mary and Martha were weeping. Lazarus was dead; four days dead. For them all hope was lost.

LESSON 6: *The Resurrection and the Life*

But Jesus knew about resurrection. Jesus knew he was Lord of life and Lord over death. Jesus knew that in a few minutes he would call Lazarus out from the grave. I don't think Jesus wept because Lazarus was dead. After all, Jesus knew about resurrection and life.

Verse 33 says, "When Jesus saw her weeping, and the Jews who had come along with her also weeping, he was deeply moved in spirit and troubled." Jesus did not weep because Lazarus was dead. From Jesus' point of view, death was not final. Lazarus would be alive again soon. Jesus wept because he saw the grief of Mary and the others, and he hurt for them. It broke his heart that their hearts were broken. He wept because they wept.

As believers, we can have confidence that Jesus has power over death. We believe death has been defeated at the resurrection of Christ. Jesus' power was demonstrated in the raising of Lazarus. So we can have hope. But it does not keep us from grieving. As the Apostle Paul said, we grieve, but not like unbelievers who have no hope (1 Thessalonians 4:13). We have hope. But we grieve nevertheless.

Jesus grieves with us. He does not grieve because our loved ones are dead. To Jesus, they are not dead at all; they are more alive than ever. But he grieves because we grieve. His heart is broken because our hearts are broken.

There is nothing wrong with having a broken heart. I find comfort in knowing that Jesus weeps with us because he cares about us. But even though we grieve, we grieve with hope because we know that Jesus is the source of resurrection life.

All for the Glory of God (11:38–44)

It seemed insensitive of Jesus not to arrive in time to save Lazarus from his illness. He could have kept Lazarus from dying. But Jesus' purpose was bigger than saving Lazarus from experiencing death. His purpose was to reveal the glory of God.

Jesus approached the tomb. In those days the dead were laid in a small cave with a stone rolled over the entrance to discourage robbers and animals. The corpse was left in the cave for about a year. Then family members would re-enter the cave, gather the bones, and place them in a small box called an ossuary. It sounds morbid to us, but it was the custom of that day.

Jesus ordered the stone to be taken away from the entrance of the tomb after Lazarus had been dead for four days. This alarmed Martha since the body would have begun the natural process of decay by this time. But once again, Jesus knew what he was doing. He was going to show them the glory of God.

Then Jesus prayed. He did not pray for God to raise Lazarus; he already knew he was Lord over death. He prayed a prayer of thanksgiving. He prayed aloud, not so

LESSON 6: *The Resurrection and the Life*   107

God would hear him, but so others around him would give glory to God and believe when they saw God's work. This was the greater purpose Jesus had in mind. *His purpose was God's glory.*

He called out to the dead man. Lazarus came walking out of the grave. It is not hard to imagine the reaction of the people who saw it. Many of them must have believed. The following verses in the background text indicate some still did not believe. They were jealous and plotted to kill Jesus. Little did they know that their actions would precipitate another resurrection that would give resurrection life to all who believe!

We may wonder why Jesus does not raise our loved ones from the grave today. We wish he would. But that is not in God's purpose. Jesus raised Lazarus as a sign of who he is. He is Christ the Lord. He is Lord of life and Lord over death. It is not necessary to have resurrections every day to believe who Jesus is. It is not necessary to see miracles like this every day to glorify God. Jesus has proven who he is, and we can believe and glorify God because we know he is the resurrection and the life.

Implications for Life

All of us have, or will, stand beside the grave of someone we love. It is always a time of grief. There is nothing wrong with that. Grief is a natural reaction to death.

But believers have hope, even in the face of death. First we find comfort because we can rest assured that Jesus weeps with us. He is not worried about our believing loved one who has departed this world. Jesus is Lord over death and knows that our loved one is more alive than ever before. But he weeps with us because he cares about those of us who grieve. We have a savior who grieves because we grieve.

Second, we have hope because we can believe in resurrection and life. We know that even though a loved one is gone from our sight, they are still enjoying the resurrection life Jesus provides. We may not understand everything about eternal life. It is a mystery to those of us who still live on this side of the grave. But we can have faith that Jesus sees better and bigger than we do. We can rest in the fact that God is taking care of our loved ones, even in death.

Finally, we can glorify God in all circumstances. Death cannot defeat God. God proved that when Lazarus was raised. Even more, God proved it when Jesus rose from the dead.

Special Friends of Jesus

Mary, Martha, and Lazarus seem to have been special friends of Jesus. The name "Lazarus" is a shortened form of the name "Eleazer," which means "One whom God helps." This Lazarus should not be confused with the Lazarus who was a character in one of Jesus' parables (Luke 16:19–31). Lazarus is not mentioned in any of the other Gospels. He does appear again in John 12, alive and well. Mary and Martha appear in Luke 10:38–42. Jesus is at their home. Martha played the busy hostess while Mary sat and listened to Jesus, much to Martha's annoyance. It appears that Jesus stayed at their house in Bethany during the last week of his life.

WORDS OF HOPE

Imagine you were asked to speak at the funeral of a friend. The family has asked that you read from John 11 and share a few words of hope from this passage. What could you say?

QUESTIONS

1. Discuss a time when you desperately needed Jesus to save the day, but Jesus seemed nowhere to be found. How did that make you feel? Did it challenge your faith? How did you respond?

2. Why do you think Jesus does not raise the dead for us today?

3. When Martha and Mary told Jesus that Lazarus would not have died if he had been there, do you think it was a rebuke or a statement of faith? Why?

4. Read the rest of Chapter 11. The religious leaders of the day plotted to kill Jesus after the raising of Lazarus. Discuss why they were anxious to get rid of Jesus, especially after this miracle.

UNIT TWO
Jesus' Private Ministry (3+ Days)

Unit Two, "Jesus' Private Ministry" contains six lessons covering roughly three-and-a-half days during the Passion week as Jesus spent intimate times of instruction, encouragement, preparation, and comfort with his disciples. In lesson seven Jesus modeled his command for us to love one another through a humble act of service. Lesson eight finds Jesus offering his disciples words of comfort while reminding them that he is the only way to the Father. In lesson nine the analogy of the vine and the branches is used to show how abiding in Christ produces a fruitful life of love and obedience. Lesson ten shows the great sacrifice made by Jesus as he completed the requirements for our redemption by dying on a cross for our sin. Through the experience of the disciples, we see how Jesus' resurrection empowers us with faith to overcome our fears and doubts in lesson eleven. The story of Peter's restoration in lesson twelve reminds us that though we may stumble, our individual responsibility to follow Jesus endures.

UNIT TWO: JESUS' PRIVATE MINISTRY (3+ DAYS)

Lesson 7	The Full Extent of His Love	John 13:1–17; 31–38
Lesson 8	The Way, the Truth, and the Life	John 14:1–14
Lesson 9	Apart From Me You Can Do Nothing	John 15:1–17
Lesson 10	It is Finished	John 19:28–42
Lesson 11	Stop Doubting and Believe	John 20:10–31
Lesson 12	Follow Me!	John 21:1–25

FOCAL TEXT
John 13:1–17; 31–38

BACKGROUND
John 13:1–38

LESSON SEVEN
The Full Extent of His Love

MAIN IDEA

Jesus modeled his command for us to love one another through a humble act of service.

QUESTION TO EXPLORE

How can we imitate Jesus' example of love for others through humble acts of service?

STUDY AIM

To choose to imitate Jesus' example of love for others through humble acts of service

QUICK READ:

As Jesus prepared the disciples for his impending death, he demonstrated love through a humble act of service.

Introduction

I could hardly wait to get to work. This day would begin my first job as a legal secretary. The town was small and I had been hired to work for the only lawyer who practiced there. The office consisted of two main rooms, his office and my front office where I intended to proudly display my skills of hospitality and efficiency.

Arriving with great anticipation, I took my shorthand pad (this was many years ago) and sat across from his desk, pen in hand, ready to take his important dictation. "Ms. Warren," he began, "the first thing I want you to do every morning is . . . clean the toilet." My incredulous and dumbfounded look must have slightly amused him. He then explained, "We are having some sewage problems and it tends to back up into the commode every night." And, for two years, I cleaned the toilet every morning.

That pride-crushing assignment was probably not my first lesson in humility, and it hasn't been and won't be the last, but it is one I will always remember. I had big plans and expectations of how to serve my new boss as the best secretary he ever had. His needs, however, did not match my elevated views of my position.

Jesus' disciples were ready to die for him. Instead, he wanted them to wash dirty feet in his name, and to act as servants rather than saviors and deliverers. Many people need deliverance from a wide variety of difficulties. These include the grip of despair, hopelessness, poverty of spirit and material goods, abuse, neglect, fear, and guilt to name only a few. Could it be their greatest need is for someone to care enough to bend down and wash their aching feet? Or hold their limp hands? Or feed their hungry children? Or sit in the hospital waiting room with them?

Jesus may have left his greatest legacy that night with his disciples: love revealed through humble service. He modeled it, and then gave two explanations for his humble act of service. Let's dig a little deeper into what Jesus was doing when he knelt at the feet of his disciples with a towel in his hands. What does he want us to hear?[1]

JOHN 13:1-17, 31-38

1 Now before the festival of the Passover, Jesus knew that his hour had come to depart from this world and go to the Father. Having loved his own who were in the world, he loved them to the end. **2** The devil had already put it into the heart of Judas son of Simon Iscariot to betray him. And during supper **3** Jesus, knowing that the Father had given all things into his hands, and that he had come from God and was going to God, **4** got up from the table, took off his outer robe, and tied a towel around himself. **5** Then he poured water into a basin and began to wash the disciples' feet and to wipe them with the towel that was tied around him. **6** He came to Simon Peter, who said to him, "Lord, are you going to wash my feet?" **7** Jesus answered, "You do not know now what I am doing, but later you will understand." **8** Peter said to him, "You will never wash my feet." Jesus answered, "Unless I wash you, you have no share with me." **9** Simon Peter said to him, "Lord, not my feet only but also my hands and my head!" **10** Jesus said to him, "One who has bathed does not need to wash, except for the feet, but is entirely clean. And you are clean, though not all of you." **11** For he knew who was to betray him; for this reason he said, "Not all of you are clean."

12 After he had washed their feet, had put on his robe, and had returned to the table, he said to them, "Do you know what I have done to you? **13** You call me Teacher and Lord—and you are right, for that is what I am. **14** So if I, your Lord and Teacher, have washed your feet, you also ought to wash one another's feet. **15** For I have set you an example, that you also should do as I have done to you. **16** Very truly, I tell you, servants are not greater than their master, nor are messengers greater than the one who sent them. **17** If you know these things, you are blessed if you do them."

• • • • • • • • • • • • • • • • • • •

31 When he had gone out, Jesus said, "Now the Son of Man has been glorified, and God has been glorified in him. **32** If God has been glorified in him, God will also glorify him in himself and will glorify him at once. **33** Little children, I am with you only a little longer. You will look for me; and as I said to the Jews so now I say to you, "Where I am going, you cannot come.' **34** I give you a new commandment, that you love one another. Just as I have loved you, you also should love one another. **35** By this everyone will know that you are my disciples, if you have love for one another."

36 Simon Peter said to him, "Lord, where are you going?" Jesus answered, "Where I am going, you cannot follow me now; but you will follow afterward." **37** Peter said to him, "Lord, why can I not follow you now? I will lay down my life for you." **38** Jesus answered, "Will you lay down your life for me? Very truly, I tell you, before the cock crows, you will have denied me three times."

When Love Becomes Personal

For the first half of this series, and the first twelve chapters of John, Jesus preached and ministered in public. He called his twelve disciples out of a larger group of followers and taught them along the way. For the most part they were observers and witnesses of his ministry to others. They had few times alone with Jesus.

The second half of the book of John focuses on a change in the direction of Jesus' life on earth. The miracles, the sermons from the mountains and lakes, and the warnings to the Pharisees came to an end. In the next chapters John described an intimate meal Jesus shared with his most devoted followers. He instructed them in the meaning of what they were about to witness in his death and resurrection. Most of them would not understand until after the resurrection, but then they would remember and comprehend all that he had said to them.

Whoa! Not My Feet! (13:1–11)

John described a meal which took place on the night before the Passover feast. The other three Gospel writers described the actual Passover meal. Regardless of the timing, this was the Last Supper for these disciples and it would turn their world upside down. Jesus would predict his betrayal by one of their group and explain the coming of the Holy Spirit. Surely when they left that supper table to walk with Jesus across the Kidron Valley to the Garden of Gethsemane where Judas would betray him, their heads were spinning. Could that be one reason Jesus began the supper with a humble act of love and personal touch?

The custom of the day was for a servant or slave to greet guests at the door of the master's home and wash the dust or mud from their feet. Sandals were the typical footwear and the roads were dusty in the summers and muddy in the winters. This home was a borrowed

LESSON 7: *The Full Extent of His Love*

one and apparently there was no servant available. The disciples probably would have been more than willing to wash Jesus' feet, but given the strife they were in regarding who was the greatest among them (Luke 22:24), they were certainly not likely to wash one another's feet.

Imagine their chagrin and humiliation when Jesus rose from the table, took off his outer robe (showing humility) and tied a towel around his waist (displaying a servant's heart). Surely they were all embarrassed, but as always Peter spoke first. I can only imagine Peter pulling his feet back under him as he resisted this humble act from Jesus. At this point, Jesus offered his first explanation as to why he was washing their feet.

Jesus was about to humble himself to death on a cross. If Peter and the others could not become humble enough to receive his washing of their feet, then pride would keep them from sharing in the glory of his death and resurrection. "Unless I wash you, you have no share with me" (John 13:8b). In no way was this sanctioning the act of footwashing as a sacrament. Neither was it referring to salvation. Rather, Jesus was pointing out to Peter, and no doubt to the others listening, that if they were to share in his fellowship and glory, they must also share in his humiliation. These men would be filled with the Spirit to carry on Jesus' message after his resurrection. If they were still competing for "greatness" they would not be credible representatives or messengers.

Paying It Forward (13:12–17)

In a movie released in 2000, Haley Joel Osment played a twelve-year-old schoolboy who was given a class project for social studies. He was to come up with a plan that would change the world through direct action. He came up with a plan to "Pay It Forward" (the name of the movie) by doing a good deed for three people who in turn must each do a good deed for three more people. The deed mushroomed into a nationwide movement. However, Jesus initiated the original "pay it forward" concept when he taught his disciples, "So if I, your Lord and Teacher have washed your feet, you also ought to wash one another's feet" (John 13:14). Jesus' plan resulted in a worldwide movement called Christianity.

Whereas Jesus' first explanation to Peter was primarily a theological one, his next explanation was practical. Not only was it practical, it turned the accepted hierarchy upside down. Jesus reminded the disciples they were not greater than he who was their Lord and Teacher. If he could submit himself to wash their feet, then they could do the same. In essence Jesus was saying *whatever I have done to and for you, you must do the same for others*. Even further, Jesus said, *not only for others, but for one another*. Their competition for position must have received quite a blow with his admonition.

Interestingly, Judas was among the disciples whose feet Jesus washed. Don't you wonder how Judas felt or what was going through his mind? We are not told that he pulled his feet back or refused Jesus' act of service. Apparently by this time Judas was no longer teachable. He had a task and it had to be fulfilled. Probably the greatest act of humility on Jesus' part was when he knelt before his betrayer and washed his feet. What an act of love! We cannot follow Jesus and discriminate between friend and enemy when choosing whom to serve with love.

A "New" Commandment (13:31–35)

How can an old commandment now be new? In Leviticus 19:18 we read, "You shall not take vengeance or bear a grudge against any of your people, but you shall love your neighbor as yourself: I am the Lord." Or how can a New Testament commandment given by Jesus now be new? When asked by a scribe which commandment was first of all, Jesus went on to give him a second one (quoting Leviticus), "You shall love your neighbor as yourself" (Mark 12:31a).

When Jesus issued this "new" commandment, he was speaking to those to whom he had just demonstrated love, and those for whom he was about to die. There would be a new order, under a new covenant. From this time forward his followers should love one another "Just as I have loved you" (John 13:34b). He showed the way, through humble acts of service one to another.

Jesus stated that love would be the distinguishing difference between his disciples and those of any other. About 100 years after John wrote his Gospel, Tertullian, a third-century church father, wrote what the pagans were saying about the Christians: "See," they say, "how they love one another . . . see how they are ready even to die for one another."[2]

Sacrifice of Love (13:36–38)

Throughout all four Gospels, Peter stood out as both follower and leader. At times he followed Jesus, yet at other times he tried to get ahead of Jesus (Matthew 17:1–4; Mark 8:31–33). Once again, Peter declared his intention to follow Jesus even though he did not know where he was going. His insistence increased to a declaration of sacrifice for Jesus, "I will lay down my life for you" (13:37b).

No doubt Peter made all these rash statements and promises out of his love for Christ. He knew Jesus had said a good shepherd would lay down his life for his sheep. He was willing to go where Jesus was going. He did not understand, however, that Jesus was going to the cross to die. Jesus had to tell a heartbroken Peter when push came to shove, that on that very night he would deny him three times.

Peter, well-intentioned, tried to show his love by vowing he would die for Jesus. Jesus, however, had just

LESSON 7: *The Full Extent of His Love* 125

described the love he commanded, "I give you a new commandment, that you love one another. Just as I have loved you, you also should love one another" (13:34). The new commandment of love was to live for one another and to humbly serve one another. Jesus would die to save Peter; Peter would not die to save Jesus. Peter was to *live* for Jesus instead.

For Life Today

As Christians, we are part of the new order, those who will carry on the message of Jesus Christ until his return. Jesus said the world would know that we are his disciples if we love one another. Love is not theoretical; it must be demonstrated. Performing humble acts of service for one another and for those who do not know Jesus is his prescription for love. Our world talks much about love, but only when we humble ourselves and put such talk into action will we be different. May our world today know we are Christians by our love.

Sacrificial Love

Dr. Robertson McQuilkin served as president of Columbia Bible College and Seminary in Columbia, South Carolina, for many years. His wife Muriel was a popular conference, radio, and television speaker. Dr. McQuilkin began to notice signs of her brilliant mind slipping. In the mid-1980's she was diagnosed with Alzheimer's. Dr. McQuilkin's career was strong and he was admired by many. He knew he had to make a decision: either put his wife in a nursing home, or leave his position to take care of her himself. He made the latter decision. For him, it was a matter of integrity. Many peers thought he was throwing away his career. Dr. McQuilkin, however, humbled himself to take on the role of a caregiver because of his great love for his wife. In doing so he said, "I also see fresh manifestations of God's love—the God I long to love more fully."[3]

SERVICE IDEAS

1. Offer to help serve a meal in a homeless shelter; then ask to eat with those you served.

2. Participate in a church activity in which you do not feel well-equipped or comfortable, (i.e. working in the nursery, chaperoning a youth camping trip, assisting with landscaping, or cleaning a neglected place in your church such as closets, ovens, etc.)

3. Invite someone you feel is often excluded in your church or community into your home for a meal.

4. Stay alert to possibilities to offer humble acts of service wherever you may see them—family,

LESSON 7: *The Full Extent of His Love*

community, church, missions—and determine in your heart and mind to do so.

QUESTIONS:

1. Reflect on the attitude of the disciples at the meal when they were arguing about who was the greatest. How did that attitude contrast with the very principles Jesus had been teaching and demonstrating in his ministry? How do you think Jesus felt in that atmosphere?

2. Do you think a summary of the Sermon on the Mount might have spoken to the disciples at this time? They had heard it before. Are there times when you speak God's words more than you act on them? When you speak those words, do you speak them with love or admonition?

3. Have you ever been the recipient of a humble act of love by someone whom you admired and looked up to? How did that make you feel?

4. Think of situations in which you are hesitant to humble yourself. Do you worry others will disrespect you if you do so? Why do you think you may hesitate?

LESSON 7: *The Full Extent of His Love*

5. Determine some ways to humble yourself before others in order to show them love. How could that happen with your family? At work? At church?

6. Peter made the rash statement, "I will lay down my life for you!" Think of ways in which you could lay down your pride in order to better show Jesus' love to others.

NOTES

1. Unless otherwise indicated, all Scripture quotations in lessons 7–9 are from the New Revised Standard Version Bible.
2. Tertullian, *Apology*, 39, cited in Bruce, *The Gospel & Epistles of John*, 294.
3. R. McQuilkin, "Living by Vows," *Christianity Today* 35 (Oct. 8, 1990) 38–40, as cited in Burge, *The NIV Application Commentary—John*, 382.

FOCAL TEXT
John 14:1–14

BACKGROUND
John 14:1–14

LESSON EIGHT

The Way, the Truth, and the Life

MAIN IDEA

Jesus is the only way to truth and eternal life with God.

QUESTION TO EXPLORE

What are some of the paths people take in seeking God?

STUDY AIM

To confidently trust Jesus as the only way to truth and eternal life with God

QUICK READ

Jesus began what is known as the Upper Room Discourse with his disciples with an assurance that he is the only way to the Father.

Introduction

Ashley grew up in an extremely dysfunctional home. She never saw her father after she was one-year-old. Her mother had three other children, two with different fathers. When she was fifteen she witnessed her mother's fatal accident. Her father died the same year. Ashley went to live with an older half-sister and her boyfriend. They took advantage of Ashley until finally she moved out on her own when she was eighteen. She had long since quit school.

No one could really blame Ashley when she felt like she had finally found someone to love and then discovered she was pregnant. Soon after her baby girl's birth, her boyfriend left too. Chrystal became Ashley's whole reason for living. She adored her little girl and proved to be an excellent young mother.

Two weeks before Chrystal's second birthday, Ashley found her early one morning in her bed—dead. Inconceivable pain gripped Ashley. For the seven months since Chrystal's death, Ashley has posted pictures of her and heartbreaking messages to her on Facebook. Many of these are "baby angel" pictures and slogans. Recently Ashley posted, "I am trying to stay strong for you, baby girl. And I'm going to try my best to be good so that I can be with you forever in heaven."

Ashley has yet to find Jesus and has yet to find comfort in his promises. Though she now desperately believes her little girl is in Jesus' arms, as do I, she does not understand

LESSON 8: *The Way, the Truth, and the Life*

that she can never be good enough to join her in heaven. Though some have tried to tell her Jesus is the only way to the Father in heaven, she has not yet grasped the truth that good works will not get her there.

Jesus told his disciples that there is a path to God for us, and that he is the only way to the Father.

JOHN 14:1–14

1 "Do not let your hearts be troubled. Believe in God, believe also in me. **2** In my Father's house there are many dwelling places. If it were not so, would I have told you that I go to prepare a place for you? **3** And if I go and prepare a place for you, I will come again and will take you to myself, so that where I am, there you may be also. **4** And you know the way to the place where I am going." **5** Thomas said to him, "Lord, we do not know where you are going. How can we know the way?" **6** Jesus said to him, "I am the way, and the truth, and the life. No one comes to the Father except through me. **7** If you know me, you will know my Father also. From now on you do know him and have seen him."

8 Philip said to him, "Lord, show us the Father, and we will be satisfied." **9** Jesus said to him, "Have I been with you all this time, Philip, and you still do not know me? Whoever has seen me has seen the Father. How can you say, "Show us the Father'? **10** Do you not believe that I am in the Father and the Father is in me? The words that I say to you I do not speak on my own; but the Father who dwells in me does his works. **11** Believe me that I am in the Father and the Father is in me; but if you do not, then believe me because of the works themselves. **12** Very truly, I tell you, the one who believes in me will also do the works that I do and, in fact, will do greater works than these, because I am going to the Father. **13** I will do whatever you ask in my name, so that the Father may be glorified in the Son. **14** If in my name you ask me for anything, I will do it."

Please Don't Go (14:1–3)

John records the beginning of Jesus' farewell discourse with his disciples in Chapter 13. Even though the disciples knew trouble was brewing in Jerusalem, they could not have been prepared for the words Jesus would begin to share with them. Last week's lesson described his beautiful act of washing their feet in preparation for his departure. The disciples had so much to take in that night as they shared what has become known as the Last Supper. The hardest point for them to grasp seemed to be in understanding that Jesus would be leaving them and going to a place they could not go.

Peter was the first, as he always seemed to be, to ask the question: "Lord, where are you going?" and "Lord,

LESSON 8: *The Way, the Truth, and the Life*

why can I not follow you now?" (John 13:36b–37a). John 14 begins with Jesus extending loving comfort: "Do not let your hearts be troubled. Believe in God, believe also in me" (14:1).

Jesus understood the turmoil and distress his disciples were feeling. He had experienced those feelings himself as he approached the grave of Lazarus (11:33); as he foretold his betrayal by Judas (13:21); and as he faced the cross (12:27). However, Jesus knew "he had come from God and was going to God" (13:3b). Now he urged his disciples to keep their faith in God and in him. In essence, Jesus told them, *keep on believing, do not give up now.* When faith is the hardest to hold on to is when we need it the most.

Jesus hastened to give his disciples even further assurance he was not leaving them behind forever. In what has become one of the most loved Scripture passages preached at funerals, Jesus assured his disciples he was leaving to go and prepare eternity for them. Since Jesus' words have been interpreted as dwelling places in most translations, his promise has often been reduced to expectations of physical mansions. In today's materialistic culture that interpretation is enticing. However, it shortchanges the vastness of Jesus' promise.

Instead of real estate, Jesus promised his disciples there would be room for all, and all those who believe would abide with him forever. He promised them, and us today, that where he is, there we will be. That should be heaven for each of us! To be with Jesus forever far outweighs what heaven looks like or where we will live.

Jesus made a very practical appeal to their faith. If he left to go prepare a place in heaven for them, he would come back to get them. The converse of that promise adds even more weight: why would he *not* come back for them? Could it possibly make sense that he would go to prepare a place for them and then never return for them? Scholars offer several interpretations of exactly when Jesus would return; most notably the Resurrection and the Second Coming. Though he returns from death at the Resurrection, that appearance does not explain having gone to his Father's house to prepare a place for his followers. The Second Coming is by far the most accepted explanation.

Only One Way, One Truth, and One Life (14:4–7)

One can almost hear the frightened frustration in Thomas' voice. He argues that if they don't know where Jesus is going, how can they possibly know how to get there? Though Jesus had spent the last three years telling them who he was and where he was going, he patiently answered with a power-packed statement that becomes (perhaps along with John 3:16) the crux of the book of John: "I am the way, and the truth, and the life. No one comes to the Father except through me" (14:6).

LESSON 8: *The Way, the Truth, and the Life*   137

These words have a rich history in the Old Testament. All three words had significant meaning for the Jews. God said to Moses, "You shall walk in all the *ways* which the Lord God hath commanded you" (Deuteronomy 5:32–33 NKJV). Isaiah said, "Thine ears shall hear a word behind thee, This is the *way*, walk ye in it" (Isaiah. 30:21 KJV). The psalmist prayed, "Teach me Thy *way*, O Lord" (Psalm 27:11 KJV). All these passages and more talked about the way; Jesus claimed to be the Way.

The psalmist declared, "Teach me thy way, O Lord; I will walk in thy *truth*" (Ps. 86:11 KJV). "I have chosen the way of *truth*," he stated in Psalm 119:30. Along with many other statements about truth in the Old Testament, Jesus now claimed to *be* the Truth. The same could be said about life. "He is in the way of *life* that keepeth instruction" (Proverbs 10:17 KJV). "Thou wilt show me the path of *life*" (Ps. 16:11 KJV). Now Jesus said, "*I am the Life.*"

I know of no better summary of what Jesus was saying in this famous statement than the words of Thomas à Kempis: "Without the way there is no going; without the truth there is no knowing; without the life there is no living. I am the way which thou must follow; the truth which thou must believe; the life for which thou must hope."[1]

A beautiful truth for us today is that Jesus is not only the way to the Father, his true destination; he is the way in which we live our daily lives. Jesus shifted his emphasis from the future to the present in John 14:7. When we take our eyes off Jesus, we will lose our way. In doing so we will find neither truth nor life. Sadly, such is the state in which Ashley (see Introduction to this lesson) is struggling today. Once she, and all of us, finds the Way, she will know the Truth, and live real Life.

One More Question—For Now (14:8–11)

To this point in Jesus' discourse we have only heard arguments and questions from Peter and Thomas. Both of those disciples were known to speak their mind. Though usually not quite so vocal, Philip chimed in at this point, "Lord, show us the Father, and we will be satisfied" (14:8). Some scholars say Jesus' answer was a rebuke and some say it was an explanation. Whatever it was, there is little doubt there was some frustration in Jesus' voice.

I find it personally satisfying when I read some of the questions recorded in the Bible. First, I often have questions myself. One day I may feel secure in my faith, but the next I may be asking for reassurance 'one more time' from Jesus. Secondly, I am comforted by the fact that Jesus, frustrated or not, answered Philip's question again. His patience and understanding far outweighed any frustration as he explained once again to Philip that he was in the Father, and the Father was in him. Perhaps Philip still didn't understand it at the time; we are not told. What he would witness in the next three days, however, should have forever settled his mind.

LESSON 8: *The Way, the Truth, and the Life* 139

Jesus asked Philip to simply put his trust in him. Just believe. John began this chapter with Jesus' words, "Believe in God, believe also in me" (14:1b). In his answer to Philip, he reverses the order. "Believe me that I am in the Father and the Father is in me" (14:11). To believe in one is to believe in the other. Faith cannot be separated between them because the Father and the Son cannot be separated.

Ask In My Name (14:12–14)

"The proof is in the pudding" was an old adage my grandmother often spoke to me. She meant I needed no other proof. If I had the pudding I had the proof. I had no idea then, and still don't, what proof was supposed to be in that pudding. Jesus gave Philip a similar option. If Philip could not place simple trust in Jesus for who he was, then Jesus implored him to look at his works. They were proof of his identity.

Jesus actually dropped a promise bombshell into his discourse at this point. Anyone who would believe in him would do even greater works! How could that be? Jesus was about to go away from the earth to his Father. This was a perfect segue into the promise he was about to give them: the promise of the Holy Spirit who would empower them (and us) to do great works. "Greater" refers to quantity, not quality.

Verses 13–14 may top the list of misunderstood sayings of Jesus. Such misunderstanding has spawned the 'name it and claim it' theology popular today. A close reading, put into context with the rest of this chapter, promises to give us anything we ask *which will glorify the Father in the Son*. Requesting a Cadillac or a luxury vacation does not meet this standard. Asking God for the power to witness to the lost does meet the criteria.

This Lesson and Life

Seeking any path to eternal life other than Jesus Christ is fruitless. Nothing will come from it and much will be lost by it. People today seek God through moral living (trying to be good enough), philosophy (reason and self-help), experience (dreams, visions), or a variety of world religions (every way leads to God). As a hospital chaplain I hear over and over when I ask a patient about his or her faith, "Oh, we're all going to the same place so it doesn't really matter" or "All roads lead to the same God." How sad!

A strong emphasis is put on exclusivity and inclusivity in our society. As Christians we are accused of being exclusive because we believe and teach Jesus is the *only Way*. Actually, the opposite is true. Christianity is more inclusive than any other religion, or non-religion. Jesus died for *everyone* and God's will is *that no one should be*

LESSON 8: *The Way, the Truth, and the Life* 141

lost. No person has to be of a certain color, nationality, gender, economic level, educational level, and the list goes on. There is no initiation. Simply believe Jesus is the Way, the Truth and the Life. What more could one want? What more can Jesus give?

RELIGIOUS BUT CONFUSED?

Jim Denison is president of the Denison Forum on Truth and Culture. In his daily Cultural Commentary on Nov. 4, 2013, he wrote: "Seventy percent of Americans who are affiliated with a religious tradition say that many religions can lead to eternal life. Even more frightening, fifty-seven percent of evangelical Protestants agree. Only among Jehovah's Witnesses and Mormons do a majority believe that their own religion is the one true faith." He goes on to say there are three "isms" which lead to this false conclusion: 1) relativism—the idea that all truth is relative and subjective; 2) pluralism—different religions are roads up the same mountain; and 3) universalism—the idea that everyone is going to heaven no matter what they believe. Our response to relativism should focus on the fact that objective truth is an intellectual and practical necessity in life. "Finally," he writes, "we can respond to universalism with the fact that Jesus is the only way to God we need, or can trust. It doesn't bother me that only one key in my pocket will start my car, so long as it works."[2]

CASE STUDY

Your friend describes her dying cousin as "the best person I've ever known." This cousin began a non-profit for women coming out of prison and dedicated most of her finances, time, and energy to see these women get a new start in life. She often allowed the children of some of the former inmates to stay in her home until their mothers could get jobs and get on their feet. When you ask about her faith, your Christian friend responds: "You know, I don't think she believes Jesus is the Son of God, but I'm sure she's going to heaven. She's too good not to." How would you respond?

QUESTIONS

1. Picture yourself at the table with Jesus the night of the Last Supper. How do you think you might have felt? What questions might you have asked Jesus?

LESSON 8: *The Way, the Truth, and the Life*

2. In a world obsessed with being tolerant and having no absolutes; how would you explain Jesus as the only way to eternal life with the Father?

3. Consider Jesus' statement that one who believes in him will do even greater works than he. Give thought to what this means in your life. What would you do for Jesus "if only you could?" How could you get started?

4. Think about all the mission work or activities you do for your church or other Christian organizations. Have you done these in your own power with ordinary results? What might happen in those same activities if you asked God, in Jesus' name, to glorify himself through Jesus?

NOTES

1. Thomas à Kempis as cited in F. F. Bruce, *The Gospel and Epistles of John* (Grand Rapids: Eerdmans Publishing Company, 1983), 299.
2. http://www.denisonforum.org/cultural-commentary/873-how-can-there-be-only-one-way-to-god. Accessed 8/29/14.

FOCAL TEXT
John 15:1–17

BACKGROUND
John 15:1–17

LESSON NINE

Apart From Me You Can Do Nothing

MAIN IDEA

Abiding in Christ produces a fruitful life of love and obedience.

QUESTION TO EXPLORE

Am I abiding in Christ and experiencing a fruitful life of love and obedience?

STUDY AIM

To understand what it means to abide in Christ and experience a fruitful life of love and obedience

QUICK READ

Only by making our home in Jesus will we glorify God. Only when we glorify God will we live out his commandment to love one another. The two cannot be separated.

Introduction

Our pastor asked me to bring the message one Sunday when he was away. I chose this passage, John 15:1–17, and spoke about staying connected to Christ. Apparently I made the topic very clear in my introduction. Little seven-year-old Grace, who had been baptized only a few months prior, leaned over to her Aunt Beth and whispered, "I haven't been a Christian long enough to be disconnected so I'm just going to color."

I still smile when I think of this story. But how do we stay connected to Jesus, the vine? And what is the result? In his Upper Room Discourse with his disciples, Jesus used an analogy of a vinegrower, a vine, and branches to emphasize the necessity to remain connected to him.

John 15:1–17

1 "I am the true vine, and my Father is the vinegrower. **2** He removes every branch in me that bears no fruit. Every branch that bears fruit he prunes to make it bear more fruit. **3** You have already been cleansed by the word that I have spoken to you. **4** Abide in me as I abide in you. Just as the branch cannot bear fruit by itself unless it abides in the vine, neither can you unless you abide in me.

⁵ I am the vine, you are the branches. Those who abide in me and I in them bear much fruit, because apart from me you can do nothing. ⁶ Whoever does not abide in me is thrown away like a branch and withers; such branches are gathered, thrown into the fire, and burned. ⁷ If you abide in me, and my words abide in you, ask for whatever you wish, and it will be done for you. ⁸ My Father is glorified by this, that you bear much fruit and become my disciples. ⁹ As the Father has loved me, so I have loved you; abide in my love. ¹⁰ If you keep my commandments, you will abide in my love, just as I have kept my Father's commandments and abide in his love. ¹¹ I have said these things to you so that my joy may be in you, and that your joy may be complete."

¹² This is my commandment, that you love one another as I have loved you. ¹³ No one has greater love than this, to lay down one's life for one's friends. ¹⁴ You are my friends if you do what I command you. ¹⁵ I do not call you servants any longer, because the servant does not know what the master is doing; but I have called you friends, because I have made known to you everything that I have heard from my Father. ¹⁶ You did not choose me but I chose you. And I appointed you to go and bear fruit, fruit that will last, so that the Father will give you whatever you ask him in my name. ¹⁷ I am giving you these commands so that you may love one another."

The True Vine (John 15:1)

"I am the true vine" is the last of the seven "I am" statements of Jesus found in the Book of John. Jesus had declared himself to be, "the bread of life" (6:35), "the light of the world" (8:12), "the gate" (10:9), "the good shepherd" (10:11), "the resurrection and the life" (11:25–26), and "the way, the truth, and the life" (14:6). All of these imageries were familiar to the Jews for each of them had a rich heritage in Israel's roots.

The bread reminded them of the manna which God provided for the Israelites in the desert. God led his people through the wilderness with a cloud by day and fire (light) by night. Sheepherding was certainly the most prominent occupation mentioned in the Psalms. The Jews definitely expected a resurrection one day. And, as was discussed in the last lesson, Jesus was the fulfillment of the way, the truth, and the life as they are used in the Old Testament. Jesus drew directly from the heart of the Jewish religion in choosing these metaphors.

The image of the vine also had a historical meaning for the Jews. Admittedly, it was not one of which they could be proud. God established the nation of Israel as his vine and expected them to produce fruit. God was the vinegrower. The vine of Israel, however, failed at every turn. In fact, every time Israel as "the vine" is mentioned in the Old Testament, it is with disfavor, heartbreak, and collapse. There are many references to Israel as the vine:

Psalms 80:8–18; Isaiah 5:1–7; Jeremiah 2:21, 12:10–11; Ezekiel 15:1–5, 17:1–6, 19:10–15; and Hosea 10:1–2. As Jews, these were familiar stories for the disciples.

Now Jesus told his disciples he was the true vine. He, as the obedient and sinless Son of God, replaced the failed vine of Israel. The Vinegrower, however, had not changed. God his Father was still the vinegrower. God had not failed Israel; Israel had failed God. In Isaiah 5:4, the prophet spoke for God when he said, "What more was there to do for my vineyard that I have not done in it?"

Empty Branches (15:2–6)

Jesus cut right to the heart of the matter with his statement, "He removes every branch in me that bears no fruit" (15:2a). Notice first that Jesus was speaking only to believers with this analogy. No one has ever been "in Christ" who denied or did not accept Christ as Savior. You cannot be removed from a place where you have never been.

Why then, would a non-fruit-bearing branch need to be removed? Without fruit, the vine would neither be recognized nor praised. Most anyone can spot an apple tree at harvest time because it is laden with apples. Many of us, myself included, would not necessarily recognize the apple tree if there were no apples on it.

Jesus talked much in his farewell discourse about glorifying the Father (John 13:31–32, 14:13, 15:8). A plant is glorified when flowers bloom from it; a fruit tree is glorified when it is laden with fruit; a vine is glorified when it produces grapes; and, God is glorified when we, as disciples, produce fruit in his name.

The wood from a vine had no other use than to bear fruit. It was too soft. This interesting fact is verified in Old Testament Scripture.

> The word of the Lord came to me: O mortal, how does the wood of the vine surpass all other wood—the vine branch that is among the trees of the forest? Is wood taken from it to make anything? Does one take a peg from it on which to hang any object? It is put in the fire for fuel; when the fire has consumed both ends of it and the middle of it is charred, is it useful for anything? When it was whole it was used for nothing; how much less—when the fire has consumed it, and it is charred—can it ever be used for anything!
>
> EZEKIEL 15:1–5

Many debates have taken place as to the meaning of the branches being thrown into the fire and burned (John 15:6). To try to take this part of Jesus' parable out of context and use it to prove the loss of salvation and burning in hell is not good scholarship. Jesus had already addressed eternal salvation in John 10:27–29. In this story he was making another point entirely. These dead branches were simply of no use to the kingdom. As Christians, we will never lose our relationship with Jesus, but we certainly can lose fellowship and thus become useless in his kingdom.

A fruit-bearing branch must still be pruned. Horticulturists will readily understand the process and need for pruning. This process produces stronger vines and a greater fruit yield. Pruning is done for the good of the growth of the plant, in this case the vine. Pruning removes anything which drains energy from the fruit-bearing branches. The word "prune" in John 15:2 is based on the same verb as "cleansed" in verse 3. Jesus assured his disciples they had been cleansed, or pruned.

Fruit is produced by the vine, not the branches. If a branch cannot produce its own fruit, then neither can we as Christians produce our own. We can give up the pressure that is so often put on us. As long as we are abiding in Christ, he will produce his fruit and show it to the world through us. Could it be that much of our busyness is spent trying to make something "spiritual" happen? I am thankful each of us does not have the responsibility to produce our own fruit. We would constantly be in competition for who produced the best. Further, we would be designing what we considered spiritual fruit. Instead, God produces in and through us the fruit he intends we should bear. God "called us with a holy calling, not according to our works but according to his own purpose and grace" (2 Timothy 1:9).

So what is the Jesus-produced fruit? Spiritual fruit will obviously consist of those characteristics mentioned in Galatians 5:22—love, joy, peace, patience, kindness, generosity, faithfulness, gentleness, and self-control. Fruit may also be others whom we lead to accept Jesus as Savior.

For most of my growing-up years in the church I was taught that new Christians were the only fruit we must be about producing. I constantly felt guilty if I was not leading someone to accept Jesus. What a relief to find that, while that is partially true, there is more. Abiding in Christ cannot help but bring forth fruit glorifying to God, be it a new Christian or a love that crosses all social, cultural, and political borders.

Jesus provided the key to bearing fruit which glorifies the Father: abide in him. Apart from him we will not produce fruit which will glorify God. We will be like a dead branch. We will detract from the kingdom, use up energy that should be used to produce fruit, and will wither. We all have dead spots from time to time—when we use our energy and our time for something other than glorifying God. Those are times we must be pruned and cleansed in order for fruit to grow. Those times often hurt, but only when we have been cleansed and forgiven can we flourish in the kingdom of God.

Taking Up Residence (15:7–11)

Abide, in my Southern dialect, simply means "stay put." Don't move away. My father was in the Air Force most of my childhood. As a result, we never stayed put. I never went to the same school more than one-and-a-half years until high school. Each time we moved we had to begin again: new school, new church, new friends, new everything. About the time we felt a part of a community, daddy got new orders and we moved. Building solid relationships was almost impossible. Today I have very few memories of people during those formative years. My husband, on the other hand, lived his entire life in one house. He still remembers classmates, neighbors, escapades, and celebrations.

I see these verses as a sweet invitation from Jesus to move in with him, live with him, and build a deep and eternal relationship with him. For the first time in this chapter he talked about love, inviting his disciples then and now to abide in his love. He gave a simple, though not always easy, instruction to accomplish this: keep my commandments. Doing so will produce the spiritual fruit of joy.

Community in Christ (15:12–17)

When I hear the phrase "keep my commandments" my mind immediately reverts to the Ten Commandments. However, Jesus spoke of the new commandment he had been talking about in his final discourse: "I give you a new commandment, that you love one another" (13:34a). He repeated this commandment almost word for word in these verses. Loving Jesus and loving one another will encompass all other commandments. Legalism will become immersed in grace.

You may remember when Jesus washed his disciples' feet he referred to them as servants and to himself as teacher and Lord. Now Jesus called them, and us, friends. God called Abraham his friend (Is. 41:8) and he spoke to Moses face to face, as one speaks to a friend (Exodus 33:11). What a promotion and what company we now keep! Psalms 103:7 states, "He made known his ways to Moses, his acts to the people of Israel." The people saw *what* God was doing, but Moses understood *why*. Jesus has called us friends because he has made known to us everything he has heard from his Father (John 15:15b). Servants are legally bound to their masters. Friends are bound to their Master by love.

Abiding in Christ Today

I serve as a hospital chaplain. When I visit patients who are near death and ask them about their family relationships, I so often hear they have children, but they are "estranged." By this they obviously mean they no longer live together (abide), but also that they have become alienated from one another. Their biological connection remains, but any fellowship has been lost. Now the end of life has arrived and they long for the closeness they once experienced. Sometimes we as chaplains are able to help such healing come about and it is a beautiful sight. Sadly however, often these relationships are irreparable.

Jesus asks that we abide (live) in him and he will abide (live) in us. Personal relationships are nurtured by time spent with one another. Likewise we must spend time with Christ, listening, conversing, crying, laughing, emulating, and, above all, obeying. From time spent in these ways will come a fruitful life which will glorify our Father in heaven. I call this a plugged-in, turned-on Christian. William Barclay describes it as a clock plugged into an electrical current rather than one running on batteries which will eventually run out. How would you describe your relationship with Jesus today?

A Primer on Viticulture

Vines were usually planted on terraces and grew so fast they had to be planted at least twelve feet apart. They covered the ground almost immediately. For at least three years a young vine was not allowed to bring forth fruit. In order for it to develop, it was cut back drastically each year. In Old Testament times, vineyards were to lie fallow every seventh year. During that time the land rested and the poor were allowed to glean from it. Pruning took place in early winter. The vines bore two kinds of branches: fruit-bearing and non-fruit-bearing. The non-fruit-bearing branches were severely and radically pruned back so they would not drain away any of the strength from the fruit-bearing branches. The vine's wood was absolutely good for nothing! It was too soft. Therefore, the only thing that could be done with the pruned wood was to make a bonfire and burn it.

Abiding in Christ

Ideas for abiding in Christ:

- Set aside a time every day; simply sit quietly and allow God to speak to you.
- Set aside a longer period once a week; choose a Scripture passage and meditate on it as you ask the Holy Spirit to teach you.

Lesson 9: *Apart From Me You Can Do Nothing*

- Try to practice a Sabbath, or a day of rest, dedicated to God. Once a month put aside work for the day and enjoy your freedom in Christ.

- Spend some quality every month with a Christian friend, celebrating your spiritual friendship.

- Make a point to let Christ's love (from the vine) grow in you (the branch) to serve someone you do not know well.

QUESTIONS

1. Think of the functions of a vinegrower, a vine, and a branch. Are there ways in which you might try to play each of these roles in your spiritual growth?

2. Based on the first question, which role is most comfortable for you to play? Which role holds the most control? Which holds the least?

3. Have you ever had an experience where something painful in your life led to greater spiritual maturity? Could that have been the Vinegrower pruning you to produce more fruit? Explain.

4. Name ways in which you knowingly abide in Christ. Solitude? Silence? Obedience? Prayer? Think of times when you have moved away from him. What brought you back to an abiding relationship with Christ?

5. Are there relationships in your life in which you play a servant role to someone with more authority or power? What is the difference between "service" and "sacrifice?" Which one deepens a friendship?

FOCAL TEXT
John 19:28–42

BACKGROUND
John 19:1–42

LESSON TEN
It is Finished

MAIN IDEA

Jesus completed the requirements for our redemption by dying on a cross for our sin.

QUESTION TO EXPLORE

What do the details of the crucifixion reveal about God's provision for us and Jesus' obedience?

STUDY AIM

To explore the details of the crucifixion and to respond to God with thanksgiving and obedience

QUICK READ

Jesus willingly took our sin upon himself and died so we could live. Realizing the pain and suffering he went through compels us to obey him and to thank him.

Introduction

If someone saves your life are you indebted to them forever? This question comes from a phenomenon in literature known as the "Life Debt." If a person saves your life you are connected to your savior's life forever. The only way to repay the debt is for you to save the life of your savior.

One reason the Gospel of John gives detailed information about Jesus' crucifixion is to show how he fulfilled Old Testament prophecy regarding the Messiah. Another reason was to describe the extreme suffering Jesus endured for us. John's Gospel uses this information to inspire us to respond to Jesus with obedience and thanksgiving.

In death, Jesus substituted his life for ours. He saved us; therefore we are indebted to him forever. We will never be able to repay our "Life Debt" to him by saving his life. But living a life of obedience to him is an excellent way to express our gratitude.

JOHN 19:28–42

28 Later, knowing that all was now completed, and so that the Scripture would be fulfilled, Jesus said, "I am thirsty." **29** A jar of wine vinegar was there, so they soaked a sponge in it, put the sponge on a stalk of the hyssop plant, and lifted it to Jesus' lips. **30** When he had received the drink, Jesus said, "It is finished." With that, he bowed his head and gave up his spirit.

31 Now it was the day of Preparation, and the next day was to be a special Sabbath. Because the Jews did not want the bodies left on the crosses during the Sabbath, they asked Pilate to have the legs broken and the bodies taken down. **32** The soldiers therefore came and broke the legs of the first man who had been crucified with Jesus, and then those of the other. **33** But when they came to Jesus and found that he was already dead, they did not break his legs. **34** Instead, one of the soldiers pierced Jesus' side with a spear, bringing a sudden flow of blood and water. **35** The man who saw it has given testimony, and his testimony is true. He knows that he tells the truth, and he testifies so that you also may believe. **36** These things happened so that the scripture would be fulfilled: "Not one of his bones will be broken," **37** and, as another scripture says, "They will look on the one they have pierced."

38 Later, Joseph of Arimathea asked Pilate for the body of Jesus. Now Joseph was a disciple of Jesus, but secretly because he feared the Jews. With Pilate's permission, he came and took the body away. **39** He was accompanied by Nicodemus, the man who earlier had visited Jesus at night. Nicodemus brought a mixture of myrrh and aloes, about seventy-five pounds. **40** Taking Jesus' body, the two of them wrapped it, with the spices, in strips of linen. This was in accordance with Jewish burial customs. **41** At the place where Jesus was crucified, there was a garden, and in the garden a new tomb, in which no one had ever been laid. 42 Because it was the Jewish day of Preparation and since the tomb was nearby, they laid Jesus there.

Jesus' Arrest, Trials, and Crucifixion (18:1–19:27)

Judas led a band of soldiers, chief priests, and Pharisees to the Garden of Gethsemane to arrest Jesus. Jesus approached them and when he told them who he was, they all fell to the ground. This demonstration of power showed that Jesus was in control. Nothing was going to happen to him that he did not will to occur.

Peter cut off the ear of the high priest's servant. Jesus rebuked him and then healed the servant's ear. Jesus was in charge. Peter did not understand the plan, so Jesus intervened.

Jesus faced hearings with both Jewish and Roman authorities. He first appeared before Annas, the father-in-law of Caiaphas the high priest. Annas questioned him and then sent him to Caiaphas. Caiaphas advised the Jewish leaders that it would be good if one man died for the people. The Jewish leaders then took Jesus to Pilate, the Roman governor.

Pilate came out of the governor's palace because the Jewish leaders would be ceremonially unclean if they entered into the Roman palace, and therefore would be ineligible to eat the Passover meal. They were more concerned with the laws of Passover than the unfair and unlawful treatment of an innocent man. The Jews wanted Pilate to execute Jesus because they were not allowed, under Roman rule, to perform executions. Under Roman captivity the Jews were given certain rights, but only the Romans could carry out a sentence of capital punishment.

The Jewish leaders declared Jesus guilty (deserving a death penalty) even before his first trial. Held at night, these illegal trials were used as a smoke screen to hide what was really happening. The Jews wanted Jesus dead. When Pilate tried to let Jesus go, the Jewish leaders threatened to report Pilate as an enemy of the Roman government. Pilate knew Jesus was innocent. He tried to appease the crowd by having Jesus beaten. The crowd would not compromise; they also wanted Jesus to die. Pilate relented to the pressure of the crowd and allowed Jesus to be crucified.

Rome crucified traitors and criminals. The Jews considered crucifixion inhumane and cursed, and did not engage in this particular practice of torture. The Jewish leaders wanted Jesus eliminated and they wanted Rome to kill him. Executioners would beat the criminal just short of death before making the condemned carry his cross beam to the execution site.

People offered the criminals a mixture of vinegar, gall, and myrrh to dull the pain of crucifixion; Jesus refused it. A small foot rest or seat was attached to the cross to enable the criminal to rest his weight on it and catch his breath. This prolonged the suffering (but was merely temporary until a later stage in the crucifixion.) Soldiers fastened criminals to the cross by pounding spikes through their wrists and ankles. This excruciating experience led to exhaustion, suffocation, brain death, and even heart failure. The soldiers broke the criminal's legs, which disabled the ability of the one crucified to push up off the cross and take a breath.

The Death of Jesus (19:28–36)

John used the Greek word *tetelestai* to reveal that Jesus knew the end was near. In verses 28–30 he uses a form of this word three times to show that Jesus realized not only his life, but also his ultimate goal, were near completion. The hour of his glorification was at hand. This was not the end of Jesus but rather the beginning of fulfilling his purpose to defeat the power of sin and death. It was a glorious moment. *Although he prayed before for the Father to remove his burden, Jesus refused to abandon his purpose.*

According to John, Jesus stated that he was thirsty. Mark recorded in his Gospel (Mark 15:23) that someone offered Jesus wine mixed with myrrh, but he did not take it. The mixture was used as a sedative to dull pain. John recorded that a person, upon hearing Jesus' statement of thirst, held up a sponge dipped in wine vinegar and put it to Jesus' lips. This act also fulfilled Scriptural prophecy. The second mixture offered was not intended to dull Jesus' pain, but was a mixture of cheap wine and vinegar, and was a favorite drink of the poorer people. This enabled Jesus to wet his lips enough to make his final pronouncement from the cross.

The question is, what Scripture was fulfilled and what was the purpose of this passage? John, in an attempt to illustrate the depth of Jesus' pain and suffering, drew upon passages in the Psalms referring to the suffering of victims facing torture. Psalm 22 is a chapter lamenting the cries of a person in pain, and in Psalm 69:3, 21, the victim suffered to the point of dehydration and was given a mixture of wine and vinegar to drink.

In John 19:30 Jesus announced "It is finished." In his account of this, John used the same word for "finished" that he used earlier in verse 28. Jesus had completed his purpose for coming to earth. At this point Jesus gave up his spirit willingly, and died. John emphasized that Jesus was a willing participant in the crucifixion story.

John wrote about the soldiers falling to the ground when Jesus spoke in the Garden of Gethsemane. Jesus also demonstrated his power over an angry mob (John 18:5–6). John again drew attention to Jesus' willing sacrifice when he told of Jesus telling Pilate that he had no power over him (John 19:11). Jesus alone declared when the battle was over (John 19:30). John again supported this claim by revealing that the soldiers did not break Jesus' legs. The two criminals hanging on either side of Jesus were fighting to hang on to life. Jesus did not fight against death, he willingly gave up his spirit.

The Romans did not usually break the legs of crucified victims. They preferred to leave a person hanging so the birds and the animals could add to the torture by eating away their flesh. However, in Jesus' case, the Jews wanted to make sure the victims were dead and removed from the cross the day before Passover. Ironically, the priests slaughtered lambs for the Passover celebration on this Day of Preparation.

Jesus knew he was the only one qualified to die for the sins of the world. Out of his love for humanity he willingly gave his life. He was God's only Son, he was sinless, he was perfect, he was innocent and yet he laid down his life for the entire world. Jesus completed his part of redemption; death. God the Father took care of the next step and raised him from the dead defeating sin, Satan, and his armies forever.

John referred to himself in the third person in verse 35 to reveal his eyewitness account of the events of Jesus' death. The fact that John witnessed these things gave evidence to claims that Jesus died and fulfilled Old Testament prophecies. John was able to later defend the validity of stories about Jesus' crucifixion and death because he was there when they happened.

The Burial of Jesus (19:38–42)

Joseph of Arimathea was a wealthy member of the Sanhedrin, the highest tribunal of the Jews. People knew of Joseph because of his wealth and high position. Most people did not know he was a disciple of Jesus. He kept this fact a secret in order to protect himself. His wealth and position allowed him to gain an audience with Pilate and he convinced Pilate to let him bury Jesus in his tomb. Joseph put his position and his life at risk with this request because it revealed him as a Jesus follower.

Normally a body was released to family members or to those who could provide a burial for the deceased. The fact that Jesus was executed for treason meant his body would not be released but rather placed in a tomb with the bodies of other criminals. Perhaps Pilate knew that Jesus was innocent of treason and thus allowed Joseph to take his body.

Nicodemus, another secret disciple of Jesus, also participated in the burial and also put his life at risk. Nicodemus provided the spices for the burial. He and Joseph wrapped Jesus' body in cloths and applied spices as customary for a Jewish burial. The amount of spices Nicodemus supplied was equivalent to the amount of spices used to bury royalty. If Jesus had been alive at this point these two men would have discovered this and stopped the burial process. They both knew Jesus was dead.

After they had prepared the body, the two men laid Jesus in the tomb owned by Joseph. The tomb was located in a garden near the place of crucifixion and the place of preparation. Matthew recorded that it was a new, unused tomb. A tomb was a valuable piece of property that families owned and used repeatedly over the years. The body of the deceased was placed on a slab inside the tomb until only the bones were left. The bones were collected and placed in a small box called an ossuary. The box was placed in another part of the tomb.

Applying This Lesson to Life

Living a life of obedience and thanksgiving is the proper response to understanding how Jesus willingly sacrificed his life for us. Although he did not have to make this sacrifice, he was the only one who could save us. Whenever we are tempted to disobey or rebel against God it is a good practice to remind ourselves of exactly what Jesus went through for us. We can never repay him for his ultimate act of love. It is not enough to simply tell Jesus thank you, we should show him our gratitude with our lives.

A Jewish Burial

The Jewish process for embalming a body was different from the Egyptian method. Egyptians removed the vital internal organs, treated them, and put them in jars. They filled the empty corpse with a mixture of spices and vinegar to slow decomposition and to hide the smell. The Jewish process was simpler. They washed the body and covered it with strips of cloth or a single piece of material. The word John used (*othoniois*) indicated they wrapped Jesus with strips of cloth. The Synoptics used the word *sindōn* indicating they used a single sheet. A single piece of linen would allow for a shroud where strips of cloth would break up the image when separated. Those preparing the body put spices around the body to cover the smell. A body would decompose much faster using this process.

THE ROMAN ROAD

Print the following Scripture references on notecards and distribute a notecard to each class member. Demonstrate how these verses can be used to share the gospel. Encourage class members to pray for opportunities to share their faith in Christ.

1. Romans 3:23
2. Romans 6:23
3. Romans 5:8
4. Romans 10:9–10
5. Romans 10:13

QUESTIONS

1. Other than the fulfillment of Scripture, what are other possible reasons John included Jesus' words, "I am thirsty"?

LESSON 10: *It is Finished* 173

2. When Jesus uttered the words "It is finished" what did he mean?

3. Why is it significant to know that Jesus went to the cross and died *willingly*?

4. Why did John give so much detail regarding Jesus' burial?

5. What did Joseph of Arimathea and Nicodemus risk by being the ones to perform Jesus' burial?

FOCAL TEXT
John 20:10–31

BACKGROUND
John 20:1–31

LESSON ELEVEN
Stop Doubting and Believe

MAIN IDEA

Jesus' resurrection empowers us with faith to overcome our fears and doubts.

QUESTION TO EXPLORE

What causes fear and doubt in my life?

STUDY AIM

To trust the resurrection power of Jesus as I face my fears and doubts

QUICK READ

Jesus' disciples feared they too would be executed. Jesus appeared to them and told them not to be afraid. Seeing his resurrected body gave them peace and removed their fear.

Introduction

Franklin D. Roosevelt stated in his first inaugural speech as president that "The only thing we have to fear is fear itself." It was 1933 and America was struggling in the grip of the Great Depression. FDR, in an effort to instill hope, reminded Americans that their common struggle centered on material things. He believed that fear had crippled Americans and stripped them of their will to succeed.

Roosevelt believed that America would rise again and overcome her present struggles. Americans just needed to see a way out. They needed someone to guide them and encourage them to advance and not to retreat in fear. Likewise, Jesus knew his followers lived in fear. He knew they needed him to calm their fears and reveal to them the victory they possessed in him.

JOHN 20:10–31

10 Then the disciples went back to their homes, **11** but Mary stood outside the tomb crying. As she wept, she bent over to look into the tomb **12** and saw two angels in white, seated where Jesus' body had been, one at the head and the other at the foot.

13 They asked her, "Woman, why are you crying?" "They have taken my Lord away," she said, "and I don't know where they have put him."

14 At this, she turned around and saw Jesus standing there, but she did not realize that it was Jesus.

15 "Woman," he said, "why are you crying? Who is it you are looking for?" Thinking he was the gardener, she said, "Sir, if you have carried him away, tell me where you have put him, and I will get him."

16 Jesus said to her, "Mary."

She turned toward him and cried out in Aramaic, "Rabboni!" (which means Teacher).

17 Jesus said, "Do not hold on to me, for I have not yet returned to the Father. Go instead to my brothers and tell them, 'I am returning to my Father and your Father, to my God and your God.'"

18 Mary Magdalene went to the disciples with the news: "I have seen the Lord!" And she told them that he had said these things to her.

19 On the evening of that first day of the week, when the disciples were together, with the doors locked for fear of the Jews, Jesus came and stood among them and said, "Peace be with you!"

20 After he said this, he showed them his hands and side. The disciples were overjoyed when they saw the Lord.

21 Again Jesus said, "Peace be with you! As the Father has sent me, I am sending you." **22** And with that he breathed on them and said, "Receive the Holy Spirit. **23** If you forgive anyone his sins, they are forgiven; if you do not forgive them, they are not forgiven."

24 Now Thomas (called Didymus), one of the Twelve, was not with the disciples when Jesus came. **25** So the other disciples told him, "We have seen the Lord!"

But he said to them, "Unless I see the nail marks in his hands and put my finger where the nails were, and put my hand into his side, I will not believe it."

26 A week later his disciples were in the house again, and Thomas was with them. Though the doors were locked, Jesus came and stood among them and said, "Peace be with you!" **27** Then he said to Thomas, "Put your finger here; see my hands. Reach out your hand and put it into my side. Stop doubting and believe."

28 Thomas said to him, "My Lord and my God!"

29 Then Jesus told him, "Because you have seen me, you have believed; blessed are those who have not seen and yet have believed."

30 Jesus did many other miraculous signs in the presence of his disciples, which are not recorded in this book. **31** But these are written that you may believe that Jesus is the Christ, the Son of God, and that by believing you may have life in his name.

Jesus Calms Mary Magdalene (20:10–18)

John intertwined his story with Mary Magdalene's at the tomb to show that Jesus appeared to both men and women. Mary was the first person to see Jesus after his resurrection. In those days the testimony of a woman did not carry much weight. However, she could confirm Peter and John's story as well as provide information about her encounter with the resurrected Christ. Mary saw Jesus at the tomb and once again he removed her fear.

Mary's first encounter with Jesus had changed her life (Luke 8:2). Jesus removed Mary's fear by casting seven demons out of her. Mary was afraid when she saw the empty tomb because she did not know what had happened to Jesus' body. He appeared to her in resurrection form and removed her doubts and fears. As a result, Jesus made her a messenger of the truth.

Mary originally feared that Jesus had not received a proper burial. Burial was a significant part of the Jewish faith. Tampering with a dead body meant tampering with the faith. Through her tears Mary peered into the tomb and saw two angels seated on the vacated slab.

It is highly unlikely Peter would have overlooked the presence of angels in the tomb. It is more likely that they appeared after Peter and John had left the graveside. One of the duties assigned to angels was to appear at crucial times and announce God's plan. Angels appeared to Mary and Joseph to announce the coming of Jesus; they appeared to the shepherds to announce the arrival of Jesus, and now at the tomb they announced to Mary what had happened to Jesus.

She turned to begin searching for his body. Then Jesus appeared, but she did not recognize him. Perhaps her eyes were blurred with tears, maybe it was too dark, or perhaps Jesus looked different in his resurrected state. Although some of his followers did not recognize him immediately when he appeared to them, once Jesus revealed his identity, he also removed their fears.

Jesus spoke to Mary and called her "woman," but she still did not recognize him until he called her by name. Mary had heard Jesus teaching the disciples about how he would die and on the third day rise from the dead. Before this moment Mary had not considered the possibility that Jesus was alive. Jesus did not scold her for her unbelief. He called her by name which revealed he knew her, and that he wanted to calm her fears. Although Jesus had changed, his relationship with Mary had not changed.

Knowing someone by name indicates intimacy and familiarity. Mary did not encounter a messenger, she encountered Jesus. Jesus knows the name of his followers. He is engaged in a personal and intimate relationship with those who believe in him. Mary was surprised and overwhelmed to see Jesus. Realizing it was Jesus, she called him her Master; her Teacher. She used a term of respect. Mary had no doubt it was Jesus. However, Jesus was more than her teacher; he was her Savior and Lord.

Apparently Mary tried to hug Jesus, but he told her not to touch him. This statement sounds harsh. It is not clear why Jesus told Mary not to hold on to him. Jesus made it clear however to Mary and the others, that they would no longer relate to him through their physical senses but rather in spirit. Mary and the others needed to learn to follow him by faith rather than by sight. Soon he would ascend into heaven and they would not be able to touch him or see him. It was clear Jesus did not allow Mary to control him, but he invited her to acknowledge him.

Jesus Calms the Disciples (20:19–22)

The disciples hid in fear. They feared they would be arrested and executed. The disciples, except for Thomas, huddled together in the darkness of the night to discuss what to do next. They met the evening of the first day of the week (Sunday), which would later be called the Lord's Day. The day started out as a day of fear and trembling for the disciples, but Jesus changed it into a day of celebration. Jesus knew they were afraid and used his first words to calm their fear, "Peace be with you!" (20:19b).

An appearance of God or Christ in the Old Testament is known as a Theophany or Christophany (see Isaiah 6). These consisted of an appearance which typically caused fear, a statement from God to not be afraid, and concluded with a commission. It was a common belief that humans could not see God and live. Jesus wanted to comfort his disciples and to prepare them for their mission.

John explained in verse 19 that the disciples were behind locked doors. This indicated the degree to which the disciples feared for their lives. The locked doors also added to the supernatural appearance of Jesus. He did not walk through the doors but suddenly appeared in the room. Jesus, in his resurrected state, had the ability to appear and disappear. However, he was not a ghost but actual flesh and blood. Perhaps Jesus allowed them to see his wounds in order to add evidence to their testimony that he was truly alive. The fact they saw him is still used today to defend Jesus' resurrection.

Verse 21 introduces the commission to the disciples to carry out the mission Jesus started. Jesus stated that in the same manner that the Father had sent him to earth to save the world, Jesus was sending his disciples. Therefore, God's mission to save people is not merely in the hands of humans, but involves a cooperative relationship between God and his followers. The peace that Jesus offered during this encounter was not only to calm their fears, but also to prepare them to receive the details of their God-sized mission.

In verse 22 John recorded that Jesus breathed on the disciples and gave them the Holy Spirit. This conflicts with Luke's later account of the Holy Spirit filling the disciples at Pentecost (Acts 2:1–4). Various interpretations exist regarding John's record. One is that the Holy Spirit came temporarily to prepare the disciples for Pentecost. Another interpretation states that the disciples received a spiritual endowment. Still another view interprets Jesus' words as symbolic of the arrival of the Holy Spirit.

The most logical explanation is that John was writing with the larger picture in mind. He grouped his writing about Jesus' commission, the preparation of the disciples, and the coming of the Holy Spirit at Pentecost in the same stream of thought. He was not concerned with chronological sequences. John revealed that Jesus, along with the Father, had the authority to send the Holy Spirit. Thus he showed the union between the Father and the Son.

Keep in mind John was writing to the church and not to individuals. The duty of the church is not to forgive sins, but rather to proclaim the forgiveness of sins through the power of Jesus' death and resurrection. Jesus commissioned his followers, the church, to identify sin and to point sinners to him for forgiveness. The church must be authentic about the struggle against sin and live in a way which makes the gospel clear, so people will have no doubt about where they stand in regards to sin. Jesus commissioned the church to proclaim forgiveness of sins in his name and to help people turn their focus from the guilt of sin to the joy of living a godly life.

Jesus Assured Thomas (20:24–31)

Thomas was not with the other disciples when Jesus initially appeared. He demanded physical proof before he would believe. Eight days later on the Lord's Day, behind locked doors, Jesus again appeared to the disciples, including Thomas. Jesus greeted the band with the familiar words "Peace be with you!" (20:26b).

Imagine the look on Thomas' face when Jesus approached him to confront his doubt. Jesus allowed Thomas to touch his wounds. Thomas had demanded earlier that he would not believe in the risen Christ unless he touched his wounds. Jesus granted his request. The fact that Jesus wanted to convince Thomas he was alive showed how Jesus desired authentic belief from his followers. This event empowered Thomas and the others to proclaim the risen Lord.

This chapter closes with a purpose statement. Verse 31 declares that the purpose of John's account was for people to believe in Jesus and receive eternal life. For John, only the dynamic belief that Jesus is God's Son and the Christ is adequate for salvation.

Apply This Lesson To Life

Jesus appeared in an hour of darkness behind locked doors to calm the disciple's fear. It is natural when we are afraid to feel trapped or in the dark. During those times we long for light and freedom. Jesus, through his presence, not only spoke peace; he brought peace. Jesus and fear cannot share the same space. Identify your fears. Write them down. One by one speak them out loud as you mentally hand them to Jesus. Tell another believer about your fears and ask them to pray for Jesus to fill that space in your life with trust. In so doing fear must flee.

HUNGER

Many fears exist in our world today that distort and destroy life as God intended. One fear in our country that is easily overlooked is hunger. Texas Baptists, under the leadership of the Christian Life Commission, are fighting to remove this fear.

Here are some hunger stats:

1. One-half of the world's population exists on less than $2 a day.
2. There are 12.4 million hungry children in America.
3. Women make up sixty percent of those chronically hungry.
4. The poverty rate in Texas is twenty-five percent higher than the national average.
5. Twenty-seven percent of Texans report having difficulty providing food for their families.
6. Ten of the thirty poorest counties in the U.S. are in Texas.

You can get involved in removing the fear of hunger in both Texas and the world through Texas Baptists. Find out more at hungeroffering.texasbaptists.org.

CASE STUDY

Imagine you are sitting at the local coffee shop reading your Bible. A man appears out of nowhere, sees you reading the Bible, and asks you if you believe that nonsense that Jesus died and came back to life. Next he asks you what evidence you have for your belief. What would you say to this man?

QUESTIONS

1. What causes fear and doubt in your life?

2. Is there any evidence that the religious leaders were searching for the disciples of Jesus?

3. What does fear do to us?

4. How does Jesus' presence remove fear?

5. What evidence do you need that Jesus can conquer anything that causes fear?

FOCAL TEXT
John 21:1–25

BACKGROUND
John 21:1–25

LESSON TWELVE
Follow Me!

MAIN IDEA

Though we may stumble, our individual responsibility to follow Jesus endures.

QUESTION TO EXPLORE

How can I maintain my focus on following Jesus in spite of my failures?

STUDY AIM

To accept Jesus' offer of restoration and to commit to following his plan for my life

QUICK READ

Jesus approached Peter on the shore of the Sea of Galilee to restore him and reinstate him to the mission. Jesus forgave Peter for denying him and gave him a mission that would change the world.

Introduction

Have you ever promised God something, but later went back on your word? Have you ever felt unworthy to follow God because of your mistakes? Have you ever doubted that you could follow God's plan for your life because of your past failures? What did you think? How did you feel?

Jesus' disciples failed him in a big way, especially Peter who denied him three times. After his resurrection, Jesus restored not only peace in the disciples' lives, but also confidence. He did this through personal encounters that restored his disciples and led them to lead lives of total commitment to his mission. After Jesus forgave and restored the disciples, many of them surrendered their lives in following him.

Our desire to follow Jesus does not exempt us from failure. Our human nature still battles our spiritual nature. Although our spiritual nature is stronger, we often give in to our human, sinful nature. A true commitment to Jesus includes perseverance and determination, even after failure. Following Jesus requires a daily commitment. We cannot stop following him because we have blown it. We may give up on God sometimes, but he never gives up on us!

LESSON 12: *Follow Me!*

JOHN 21:1–25

1 Afterward Jesus appeared again to his disciples, by the Sea of Tiberias. It happened this way: **2** Simon Peter, Thomas (called Didymus), Nathanael from Cana in Galilee, the sons of Zebedee, and two other disciples were together. **3** "I'm going out to fish," Simon Peter told them, and they said, "We'll go with you." So they went out and got into the boat, but that night they caught nothing.

4 Early in the morning, Jesus stood on the shore, but the disciples did not realize that it was Jesus.

5 He called out to them, "Friends, haven't you any fish?"

"No," they answered.

6 He said, "Throw your net on the right side of the boat and you will find some." When they did, they were unable to haul the net in because of the large number of fish.

7 Then the disciple whom Jesus loved said to Peter, "It is the Lord!" As soon as Simon Peter heard him say, "It is the Lord," he wrapped his outer garment around him (for he had taken it off) and jumped into the water. **8** The other disciples followed in the boat, towing the net full of fish, for they were not far from shore, about a hundred yards. **9** When they landed, they saw a fire of burning coals there with fish on it, and some bread.

10 Jesus said to them, "Bring some of the fish you have just caught."

11 Simon Peter climbed aboard and dragged the net ashore. It was full of large fish, 153, but even with so many the net was not torn. **12** Jesus said to them, "Come and have breakfast." None of the disciples dared ask him, "Who are you?" They knew it was the Lord. **13** Jesus came, took the bread and gave it to them, and did the same with the fish. **14** This was now the third time Jesus appeared to his disciples after he was raised from the dead.

15 When they had finished eating, Jesus said to Simon Peter, "Simon son of John, do you truly love me more than these?"

"Yes, Lord," he said, "you know that I love you."

Jesus said, "Feed my lambs." **16** Again Jesus said, "Simon son of John, do you truly love me?" He answered, "Yes, Lord, you know that I love you." Jesus said, "Take care of my sheep."

17 The third time he said to him, "Simon son of John, do you love me?"

Peter was hurt because Jesus asked him the third time, "Do you love me?" He said, "Lord, you know all things; you know that I love you."

Jesus said, "Feed my sheep. **18** I tell you the truth, when you were younger you dressed yourself and went where you wanted; but when you are old you will stretch out your hands, and someone else will dress you and lead you where you do not want to go." **19** Jesus said this to indicate the kind of death by which Peter would glorify God. Then he said to him, "Follow me!"

20 Peter turned and saw that the disciple whom Jesus loved was following them. (This was the one who had leaned back against Jesus at the supper and had said, "Lord, who is going to betray you?") **21** When Peter saw him, he asked, "Lord, what about him?"

22 Jesus answered, "If I want him to remain alive until I return, what is that to you? You must follow me." **23** Because of this, the rumor spread among the brothers that this disciple would not die. But Jesus did not say that he would not die; he only said,"If I want him to remain alive until I return, what is that to you?"

24 This is the disciple who testifies to these things and who wrote them down. We know that his testimony is true.

25 Jesus did many other things as well. If every one of them were written down, I suppose that even the whole world would not have room for the books that would be written.

What a Fish Story! (21:1–14)

The Gospel of Mark reports that an angel at the tomb told Mary to go and tell the disciples Jesus was going ahead to Galilee to meet with them (Mark 16:6–7). John, in chapter 21 of his Gospel, told the story of Jesus appearing to the disciples by the Sea of Galilee.

Scholars disagree on why Peter and some of the other disciples were fishing. Some believe they were running away, others think they were going back to their previous occupation before meeting Jesus. Because the angel instructed them to go to Galilee to find Jesus, it is logical they were passing the time, or even fishing to have something to eat until Jesus arrived. After all they loved to fish and could use the time to reflect.

John listed seven disciples on the boat with him that day. The group included Simon Peter, who was the leader. Thomas, known as the "doubter," was there (John described him in chapter 20). By listing Thomas, John showed the connection between chapters 20 and 21. Nathanael was also present. When he first met Jesus, the Lord declared that Nathanael was an Israelite in whom there was nothing fake (1:47). The other Gospel writers did not include Nathanael in their list of the twelve disciples. However, John lists him here as coming from Cana in Galilee. Next he listed James and John, the sons of Zebedee. They are not mentioned anywhere else in John's Gospel. Finally John listed two unnamed disciples.

John set the scene to highlight another miracle performed by Jesus. The men had fished all night and caught nothing. Night was typically a great time to fish on the Sea of Galilee. Those on the boat were experienced fishermen and the fact that they had not caught any fish was unusual.

John reported that it was morning, the beginning of a new day and a new era for Christianity. Jesus called out to the disciples and used a term that can mean either "children" or "friends." It is a term of intimacy used to describe a relationship between a parent and a child, or a follower and a leader. Jesus asked them if they had caught anything to eat. They replied no. Jesus told them to cast their nets on the right side of the boat. Greeks believed that the right side of anything was good luck. The real question is why did they follow a stranger's instructions?

The disciples had yet to recognize Jesus. Fishermen were used to people giving them advice on how and where to fish. John does not indicate why they tried the right side, perhaps they were so tired and frustrated they would try anything. Perhaps there was something in Jesus' voice that resonated with authority. Whatever the reason the results were miraculous.

John's story connects with Luke's story of when Jesus first called Peter to follow him (Luke 5:1–7). In like fashion Peter had fished all night but had not caught any fish. Jesus, a stranger to Peter at the time, went out on the boat with Peter and told him to drop his nets again. Peter caught a net full of fish.

In describing this post-resurrection event, John recorded the number of fish caught; 153 (John 21:11). It was like Déjà vu all over again as the disciples pulled up a net full of fish. Finally the disciples recognized the stranger on the shore. John revealed quick insight and Peter displayed quick reaction. John recognized Jesus first and Peter was the first to jump into the water to swim towards him.

The boat was not far from the shore, so the other disciples followed Peter in the boat. They arrived on shore and approached Jesus. Not one disciple tried to avoid Jesus or run from him. They were excited to see him and wanted to be near him. When they approached Jesus they found him cooking breakfast. John described a fire with burning coals. The word for "coals" is only used twice in this Gospel. Both times were connected with Peter; the first time was when he denied knowing Jesus (as he stood around a fire to warm himself), and the second time was when Jesus reinstated Peter.

John joined Luke's theme of using food to illustrate the state of Jesus' resurrected body. John showed that Jesus got hungry and that he ate after God had raised him from the dead. Jesus was in bodily form. Jesus took on the role of host and distributed the food to the disciples, just as he did during their last supper together. Finally in verse 14, John provides evidence of two other times Jesus appeared to his disciples after the resurrection.

A Personal and Purposeful Reinstatement (21:15–19)

John recorded a conversation between Jesus and Peter which proved to be significant for Peter in several ways. The conversation reinstated Peter to "follower status" and it revealed to Peter what following Jesus would require of

LESSON 12: *Follow Me!* 197

him in the future. Jesus asked Peter a series of three questions regarding his feelings and commitment to Jesus. The number three is significant because Peter had denied knowing Jesus three times.

Jesus confronted Peter's sin directly. Dealing with Peter's past sin, specifically his denial, was required for Peter to be able to fulfill his calling. Jesus knew Peter would face more persecution in the future. The church also looked to Peter for guidance and as an example of how to follow Jesus.

Jesus had heard Peter's bold declaration that he would follow Jesus to the death. Jesus heard when Peter denied knowing him for the third time. Now, Jesus needed to know that Peter was prepared to do whatever it might take to carry out the mission of the gospel. Jesus asked Peter if he loved him more than the other disciples. Peter stated that he did love Jesus. He did not address the "more than these" statement. Peter had once told Jesus he would stay with him even if the others abandoned him. He did not live up to that claim and therefore responded with humility when questioned by Jesus. He knew if he actually loved Jesus more than the other disciples.

The Greek word Jesus used for "love" is used to describe "ultimate, self-sacrificing" love. The word Peter used for "love" was a word that referred to a "friendship" type of love. Some scholars believe Jesus was attempting to get Peter to commit to superior love, but that Peter was only comfortable with a lesser expression of love. Peter, after his denial, did not have the confidence at the time that he could love Jesus at the highest level. Other scholars believe the word choice was more stylistic in nature. Regardless, it is obvious that Jesus questioned Peter to know his heart and to prepare him for greater things ahead.

Jesus asked Peter a second time if he loved him. Jesus used the same words as before and Peter responded with the same words he used before. The third time Jesus asked Peter he used the same word Peter used which referred to a "friendship" type of love. Jesus instructed Peter to prove his love. Without actions, love (like faith) is dead. Jesus reinstated Peter and gave him a task. In typical fashion, Jesus blessed Peter, called him, and gave him a mission.

Jesus used shepherding language to describe Peter's mission. John recorded earlier that Jesus referred to himself as the "good shepherd." He also gave his job description as a shepherd. One profound statement of this description was when Jesus declared that a shepherd must lay down his life for his sheep.

Jesus concluded his conversation with Peter by prophesying about how Peter would die. At the time John wrote these verses Peter had already been martyred. This statement was significant for the early church. It is commonly believed that Peter died by crucifixion. His death concerned the early church, which faced many trials and persecutions. Jesus showed that Peter's death would not be in vain, but would serve to further the cause of Christ. Peter would lay down his life for the sheep.

What About John? (21:20–25)

Peter turned and looked at John and asked about his future. Peter, realizing he would give his life in service to Christ, wanted to know if John would do the same. Jesus told Peter not to concern himself with John's future. Jesus has a specific path for each of his followers. Each path is unique but they fit into God's overall plan for eternity. Jesus wanted Peter to obey him, regardless of how others responded.

In verse 20 John referred to himself as the one who leaned on Jesus' breast at the Passover meal. This reference shows intimacy between Jesus and John. Peter encouraged John to ask Jesus a question at that supper. Peter's motive for asking Jesus about John's future could have been genuine concern. However, an understanding of Peter's personality leans more towards Peter comparing his future to John's. In other words, if Peter has to die shouldn't John have to suffer the same future?

Great debate exists as to the meaning of "We" in verse 24. It is possible that there was a community responsible for proving the legitimacy of the author's testimony. The author worked hard to hide his identity. However, the writer wanted to make sure the readers believed what was written. This verse connects with verse 20 to reveal that John is the author. John, the beloved disciple, is the one who is mentioned throughout the fourth Gospel. Jesus allowed him to experience some of the important moments of his life such as the Transfiguration, going deeper in the Garden of Gethsemane to pray, and receiving Jesus' mother Mary as his own.

Applying This Lesson to Life

John highlighted Peter as the poster-child for failing Jesus. Peter had boasted to Jesus that he would never leave him. But Peter denied knowing Jesus when confronted by an angry crowd. After the resurrection, Jesus redeemed and reinstated Peter as a leader when he met him on the shore of the Sea of Galilee.

Peter's life gives all Christ followers cause to rejoice. Believe that God has a mission for your life. When you stray from that mission or when you fail at your mission, run to Jesus and accept his forgiveness and his invitation to fulfill your purpose. Following Jesus requires a daily commitment to stay on mission regardless of our struggles or failures. Our lives are a part of a bigger picture, and God will enable us and empower us to fulfill his mission in our lives.

Shepherds

Shepherds spend most of their time taking care of sheep or goats. A shepherd's responsibility toward the sheep involves leading them to pastures where plenty of food and water exist, protecting them from predators, and mending cuts and broken bones. A shepherd is responsible for searching for sheep when they are missing. Sheep are totally dependent on the shepherd for everything. A shepherd carries few supplies for the job. In ancient days a cloak, a staff, a bag for food, and a sling were all that was required to carry out the responsibilities of a shepherd.

Ancient authors used shepherd imagery, including biblical writers. Ancient writers referred to other deities and kings and princesses as shepherds. Jesus referred to himself as the "good shepherd" in John 10:11. His responsibility was to lay down his life for his sheep. Today pastors are often referred to as shepherds, charged to care for the flock of God's people.

Case Study

Blake had wanted to be a pastor for as long as he could remember. At an early age he felt the call of God to lead people. While fulfilling his calling he got involved in counseling a woman which ultimately led to Blake committing adultery with this woman. He left the ministry, divorced his wife, and rarely sees his kids. He still believes that God wants him in ministry. Blake asks you how you feel about him going back into ministry. What do you tell him?

QUESTIONS

1. What has God created you to do?

2. How have you responded to your failures in the past?

LESSON 12: *Follow Me!* 203

3. Imagine how Jesus felt when Peter denied him three times. What possible impact did the encounter with Peter on the Sea of Galilee have on the resurrected Jesus?

4. What are possible reasons Peter swam to Jesus instead of running from him?

5. How did Jesus' commissioning of Peter to "feed his sheep" complete Peter's reinstatement?

FOCAL TEXT
Luke 1:26–45

BACKGROUND
Luke 1:26–45

CHRISTMAS LESSON

Nothing Is Impossible with God

MAIN IDEA

The angel's announcement to Mary reminds us that God is able and faithful to fulfill his promises.

QUESTION TO EXPLORE

How do we respond to messages from God we don't fully understand?

STUDY AIM

To trust God's leading in my life even when I may not fully understand it

QUICK READ

The angel Gabriel told a young virgin named Mary that she would conceive a special child from God. She humbly submitted to God's will even though she did not understand it.

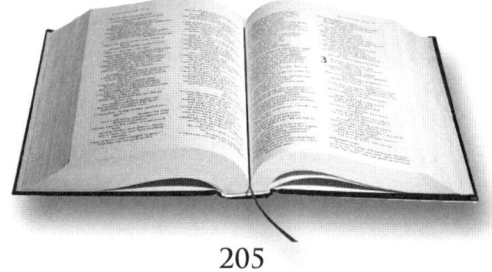

Introduction

Little Johnny was chosen to play the angel Gabriel in the annual church Christmas pageant. For weeks he rehearsed his one line: "Hail, thou that art highly favored. The Lord is with thee." When his grandparents visited he practiced on them: "Hail, thou that art highly favored. The Lord is with thee." His grandparents were so proud. The neighbors came over to the house for a Christmas party and he practiced on them: "Hail, thou that art highly favored. The Lord is with thee." He was the next Tom Hanks; everyone said so. He was ready.

The big night came for the pageant and everyone was there. Grandparents, aunts and uncles, and neighbors and friends packed into the church to see shepherds in bathrobes and angels wearing wings. The drama began with the great announcement by the angel Gabriel. The spotlight hit little Johnny, and as he stood center stage in the middle of all of the excitement, his brain stood still. Mom and Dad, grandparents and relatives, and neighbors all mouthed in unison: "Hail, thou that art highly favored. The Lord is with you." But little Johnny could not say his line. He tried, but the words would just not come out of his mouth. Finally, he filled his lungs and blurted out, "Have I got news for you!"

Indeed he did have news: ridiculous news, impossible news! It was news from God that Mary could not understand. No one could have understood the full meaning of the angel's message.

Luke 1: 26–45

26 In the sixth month, God sent the angel Gabriel to Nazareth, a town in Galilee, **27** to a virgin pledged to be married to a man named Joseph, a descendant of David. The virgin's name was Mary. **28** The angel went to her and said, "Greetings, you who are highly favored! The Lord is with you."

29 Mary was greatly troubled at his words and wondered what kind of greeting this might be. **30** But the angel said to her, "Do not be afraid, Mary, you have found favor with God. **31** You will be with child and give birth to a son, and you are to give him the name Jesus. **32** He will be great and will be called the Son of the Most High. The Lord God will give him the throne of his father David, **33** and he will reign over the house of Jacob forever; his kingdom will never end."

34 "How will this be," Mary asked the angel, "since I am a virgin?"

35 The angel answered, "The Holy Spirit will come upon you, and the power of the Most High will overshadow you. So the holy one to be born will be called the Son of God. **36** Even Elizabeth your relative is going to have a child in her old age, and she who was said to be barren is in her sixth month. **37** For nothing is impossible with God."

38 "I am the Lord's servant," Mary answered. "May it be to me as you have said." Then the angel left her.

39 At that time Mary got ready and hurried to a town in the hill country of Judea, **40** where she entered Zechariah's home and greeted Elizabeth. **41** When Elizabeth heard Mary's greeting, the baby leaped in her womb, and Elizabeth was filled with the Holy Spirit. **42** In a loud voice she exclaimed: "Blessed are you among women, and blessed is the child you will bear! **43** But why am I so favored, that the mother of my Lord should come to me? **44** As soon as the sound of your greeting reached my ears, the baby in my womb leaped for joy. **45** Blessed is she who has believed that what the Lord has said to her will be accomplished!"

The Impossible News (1:26–33)

The news was announced by the angel Gabriel. In popular belief we might think of angels as guardians who protect us from danger. But the Bible does not reveal angels as our guardians. In the Bible, angels are heralds, announcing messages from God.

The angel Gabriel fulfilled the role of a messenger. This was not the only time Gabriel announced a message. In this same chapter Gabriel announced news to Zechariah, the father of John the Baptist, that his previously barren wife Elizabeth was expecting a child. Later, angels would announce the birth of Jesus to shepherds. Matthew says it was an angel who announced to the women that Jesus was not in the tomb but alive. Angels in the Bible are not guardians; they are messengers.

Mary was betrothed to Joseph. Luke notes that Joseph was a descendent of David, an important detail in fulfilling the prophecy that the Messiah would come from the line of David. Betrothal was more serious than our modern-day engagement. It was a pledge between families that carried legal implications. Breaking of a betrothal was tantamount to divorce, unlike our customs where engaged couples can break up without legal entanglement. If Mary was pregnant it was a very serious breach of the contract and carried a severe penalty.

Betrothal, however, was not equal to marriage. Although betrothed couples were contracted to be married, a betrothed couple was expected to abstain from sexual relations until after the wedding. The Scriptures emphasize that Mary was a virgin.

Mary's virginity is what made the angel's news impossible. Gabriel told Mary she was expecting a baby and that she should name him Jesus. Mary was understandably troubled by this news. At first this did not seem like good news. News like this traveled fast in a small town like Nazareth. The angel told her she had been favored by

God, but what kind of favor was this? She must have been afraid.

But Gabriel gave her the rest of the story. He told her not to be afraid. This was a common message from angels. They almost always told people not to be afraid. The appearance of an angel would be enough to frighten anyone, but often God's message itself can strike fear in us. When God does something with us, it often turns our lives upside down. Mary knew that if this message was true it would cause trouble.

But Gabriel told her not to be afraid. God had chosen her. God had not chosen her because she was sinless. He chose her out of his sovereign will. *It was not Mary's fault; it was God's favor.* This was a special child; a ruler who would be called the Son of the Most High. Mary had been chosen by God to bear the Savior of the world!

Nothing Is Impossible with God (1:34–37)

Mary had a hard time believing the news, even though it came from an angel. "How can this be, I am still a virgin?" (1:34). It was an understandable question. Mary may have been young and inexperienced, but she knew where babies came from.

We might imagine that Mary had some other thoughts that frightened her. How was she going to explain this? This "good news" may not have been so good for Mary.

She was probably a teenager; betrothed but not married. How would she explain this to Joseph? How would the conversation go with her parents when she came down to breakfast one morning unable to hide her condition and stutter out, "Mom and Dad, I have something to tell you." Were her grandparents disappointed in her when they heard the news? Did the preacher click his tongue at her as if to say she should have been paying more attention in Sunday School the day they talked about this sort of thing? Mary knew the truth about her virtue, but would anyone else believe her?

Yet we do believe her, don't we? We believe the Holy Spirit came upon Mary to give her this child. We must be careful not to imagine some sort of mystical sexual encounter with the Spirit. The angel simply said that God had worked a miracle in her. Even though Mary may have thought no one would ever believe it, millions of Christians do believe it, even in our modern scientific age. We sing about it in Christmas carols, we claim it in creeds and confessions. Jesus was born of a virgin.

If we don't believe it, how else can we explain what Jesus turned out to be? He was human. He was born to a human mother, felt human pain, and died a human death. People who loved him could embrace him, and people who hated him could whip whelps into his back. He bled like any human being.

Yet it turns out he was God as well. Gabriel told Mary that her son would be called the Son of God. Who else could perform the miracles he did? Who else could walk on water or multiply bread and fish? At the culmination of his ministry, who else could have walked out of his own grave except God? He was fully God and fully human. It was impossible news. We don't really understand it. But the virgin birth points to the truth about Jesus.

There was more impossible news. Her relative Elizabeth was pregnant too! Gabriel had already announced this news to Elizabeth's husband Zechariah (1:5–25). Zechariah had a hard time believing it since Elizabeth had been barren for many years. But like the angel had said, nothing is impossible with God.

Responding in Faith (1:38–45)

Mary could not have understood all of what God was doing but she responded in faith. She could have gone kicking and screaming into the future, but instead she submitted to God's plan in faith and humility, even though this impossible news was incomprehensible. She understood herself to be a vessel of God whom God wanted to use to carry out his redemption plan.

Mary ran to see Elizabeth. In some way God had told Elizabeth the news about Mary. When Mary spoke, Elizabeth's baby (who turns out to be John the Baptist) jumped around in her womb. Even before he was born, John was announcing the coming of the Lamb of God!

Mary's fears must have been calmed by the welcome she received from Elizabeth. Instead of condemning Mary for being pregnant before marriage, Elizabeth rejoiced. She even proclaimed a blessing on Mary and on her child. Mary had done nothing to get pregnant. She had simply been a willing servant of God who would respond in faith to the mysterious ways of the Lord. Elizabeth recognized it as the grace of God. She rejoiced in this impossible news because she could see that God was at work.

Finally, Elizabeth commended the faith of Mary. She blessed her for believing that God was accomplishing his will. It must have been difficult for both of these women to see everything God was doing. Mary and Elizabeth could not have known at this point what the future would hold. They could not have seen the rise of John the Baptist as a great prophet who would prepare the way for the Lord. They could not have foreseen the ministry of Jesus, the cross, and certainly not the resurrection. They could not have anticipated that Jesus would save the world and have followers that would find eternal life even 2,000 years later. They could not see all of that. But they believed God was at work and they trusted him.

Implications and Actions

We have news to announce this Christmas! It is ridiculous news; impossible news.

God sent his Son into the world to save the world from sin. He was born of a virgin, lived a sinless life, died a sacrificial death, and walked out of his own grave. He was fully human and fully God.

Perhaps we cannot claim to understand all of that. It is incomprehensible to fathom God putting on flesh and living among us as a human being. We don't really understand how a virgin could give birth. It goes against every scientific and biological premise we know. We don't understand how Jesus could be one hundred percent God and one hundred percent human. We can describe it, but we cannot understand it. Yet, like Mary and Elizabeth, we can believe that God is at work. We can trust God to carry out his plan whether we understand it all or not.

Sometimes things happen in our lives we do not understand. Yet we need not be afraid. God is still working. God is still carrying out his plan. He has asked us to participate; to be willing vessels in his purpose of saving the world. May it be so.

Betrothal

The NIV says that Mary was "pledged to be married" to Joseph (Luke 1:27). They were "betrothed." Betrothal was more than an engagement but less than marriage. It was a contract between two families that may have been arranged by the parents while the children were very young, infants even. It was a way of insuring offspring for both families as well as cementing bonds between the families.

Breaking a betrothal was serious, requiring divorce. Matthew tells us that when Joseph learned of Mary's pregnancy he planned to do what the law required. The law said if a betrothed woman was unfaithful to her pledge she could be stoned or divorced. Stoning does not seem to have been very prevalent in these cases, but it was possible. Joseph was determined to quietly divorce Mary to fulfill the requirements of the law. Fortunately an angel also appeared to Joseph and assured him that this impossible news was God at work. He chose to wed Mary despite her condition.

Hard to Explain?

Pretend you are Mary. What would you say to your parents about this experience? How would you explain being pregnant to your relatives and friends?

Pretend you are Mary's parents. Would you believe her explanation of how she became pregnant? What would you say to her?

QUESTIONS

1. Use a concordance to find where the Bible mentions angels. What is the usual role of angels in the Bible? What do the appearances of angels have in common?

2. Mary responded to her impossible news with humble faith and a willingness to be used by God. What are other ways Mary *could* have responded?

3. Why is the doctrine of the virgin birth important? Can a person be a Christian if they do not believe the virgin birth? Why or why not?

4. How do you respond when God seems to be working in your life but you do not understand it?

Our Next New Study
(Available for use beginning March 2015)

EXODUS:
Liberated for Life in Covenant with God

Lesson 1	Women and Children First	Exodus 1:8—2:10
Lesson 2	Listen Up	Exodus 3:1–14; 4:1–15
Lesson 3	God's Power for God's People	Exodus 5:1–2; 6:1–8; 7:1–5, 14–18; 8:1–3, 16, 20–21; 9:1–4, 8–9, 13–18, 25–26; 10:3–11, 21–22, 28–29; 11:1–5
Lesson 4	A Hurried Meal for a Dangerous Journey	Exodus 12:1–14, 24–27; 13:8–9
Lesson 5	Questions and Faith	Exodus 14:1–4, 10–31; 15:1–2, 20–21
Lesson 6	Making Bitterness Sweet and Emptiness Full	Exodus 15:22—16:18

Lesson 7	Risking Meeting God	Exodus 19:1–12, 16–22
Lesson 8	Core Behaviors of Covenant People	Exodus 20:1–17
Lesson 9	Dealing with the Details of Covenant Living	Exodus 21:1–2, 7–17, 22–27; 22:21—23:12
Lesson 10	Seeing God	Exodus 24
Lesson 11	Earthly Things for Holy Purposes	Exodus 25:1–11, 17–18, 23–24, 31–32; 26:1–2, 7–8; 27:1–2; 29:43–46
Lesson 12	A Broken Covenant and a Fresh Start	Exodus 32:1–19, 30–33; 33:12–17; 34:1–7
Lesson 13	All for God's Service	Exodus 35:4–10, 20–35; 36:2–7
Lesson 14	Finishing and Moving On	Exodus 39:32, 42–43; 40:1–2, 16–17, 32–38
Easter Lesson	Stop Being Afraid	Matthew 28:1–10

How to Order More Bible Study Materials

It's easy! Just fill in the following information. For additional Bible study materials available both in print and online, see www.baptistwaypress.org, or get a complete order form of available print materials—including Spanish materials—by calling 1-866-249-1799 or e-mailing baptistway@texasbaptists.org.

Title of item	Price	Quantity	Cost
This Issue:			
The Gospel of John: Believe in Jesus and Live!—Study Guide (BWP001187)	$3.95	_____	_____
The Gospel of John: Believe in Jesus and Live!—Large Print Study Guide (BWP001188)	$4.25	_____	_____
The Gospel of John: Believe in Jesus and Live!—Teaching Guide (BWP001189)	$4.95	_____	_____
Additional Issues Available:			
14 Habits of Highly Effective Disciples—Study Guide (BWP001177)	$3.95	_____	_____
14 Habits of Highly Effective Disciples—Large Print Study Guide (BWP001178)	$4.25	_____	_____
14 Habits of Highly Effective Disciples—Teaching Guide (BWP001179)	$4.95	_____	_____
Growing Together in Christ—Study Guide (BWP001036)	$3.25	_____	_____
Growing Together in Christ—Teaching Guide (BWP001038)	$3.75	_____	_____
Guidance for the Seasons of Life—Study Guide (BWP001157)	$3.95	_____	_____
Guidance for the Seasons of Life—Large Print Study Guide (BWP001158)	$4.25	_____	_____
Guidance for the Seasons of Life—Teaching Guide (BWP001159)	$4.95	_____	_____
Living Generously for Jesus' Sake—Study Guide (BWP001137)	$3.95	_____	_____
Living Generously for Jesus' Sake—Large Print Study Guide (BWP001138)	$4.25	_____	_____
Living Generously for Jesus' Sake—Teaching Guide (BWP001139)	$4.95	_____	_____
Living Faith in Daily Life—Study Guide (BWP001095)	$3.55	_____	_____
Living Faith in Daily Life—Large Print Study Guide (BWP001096)	$3.95	_____	_____
Living Faith in Daily Life—Teaching Guide (BWP001097)	$4.25	_____	_____
Participating in God's Mission—Study Guide (BWP001077)	$3.55	_____	_____
Participating in God's Mission—Large Print Study Guide (BWP001078)	$3.95	_____	_____
Participating in God's Mission—Teaching Guide (BWP001079)	$3.95	_____	_____
Profiles in Character—Study Guide (BWP001112)	$3.55	_____	_____
Profiles in Character—Large Print Study Guide (BWP001113)	$4.25	_____	_____
Profiles in Character—Teaching Guide (BWP001114)	$4.95	_____	_____
Genesis: People Relating to God—Study Guide (BWP001088)	$2.35	_____	_____
Genesis: People Relating to God—Large Print Study Guide (BWP001089)	$2.75	_____	_____
Genesis: People Relating to God—Teaching Guide (BWP001090)	$2.95	_____	_____
Ezra, Haggai, Zechariah, Nehemiah, Malachi—Study Guide (BWP001071)	$3.25	_____	_____
Ezra, Haggai, Zechariah, Nehemiah, Malachi—Large Print Study Guide (BWP001072)	$3.55	_____	_____
Ezra, Haggai, Zechariah, Nehemiah, Malachi—Teaching Guide (BWP001073)	$3.75	_____	_____
Psalms: Songs from the Heart of Faith—Study Guide (BWP001152)	$3.95	_____	_____
Psalms: Songs from the Heart of Faith—Large Print Study Guide (BWP001153)	$4.25	_____	_____
Psalms: Songs from the Heart of Faith—Teaching Guide (BWP001154)	$4.95	_____	_____
Jeremiah and Ezekiel: Prophets of Judgment and Hope—Study Guide (BWP001172)	$3.95	_____	_____
Jeremiah and Ezekiel: Prophets of Judgment and Hope—Large Print Study Guide (BWP001173)	$4.25	_____	_____
Jeremiah and Ezekiel: Prophets of Judgment and Hope—Teaching Guide (BWP001174)	$4.95	_____	_____
Amos, Hosea, Isaiah, Micah: Calling for Justice, Mercy, and Faithfulness—Study Guide (BWP001132)	$3.95	_____	_____
Amos, Hosea, Isaiah, Micah: Calling for Justice, Mercy, and Faithfulness—Large Print Study Guide (BWP001133)	$4.25	_____	_____
Amos, Hosea, Isaiah, Micah: Calling for Justice, Mercy, and Faithfulness—Teaching Guide (BWP001134)	$4.95	_____	_____
The Gospel of Matthew: A Primer for Discipleship—Study Guide (BWP001127)	$3.95	_____	_____
The Gospel of Matthew: A Primer for Discipleship—Large Print Study Guide (BWP001128)	$4.25	_____	_____
The Gospel of Matthew: A Primer for Discipleship—Teaching Guide (BWP001129)	$4.95	_____	_____
The Gospel of Mark: People Responding to Jesus—Study Guide (BWP001147)	$3.95	_____	_____
The Gospel of Mark: People Responding to Jesus—Large Print Study Guide (BWP001148)	$4.25	_____	_____
The Gospel of Mark: People Responding to Jesus—Teaching Guide (BWP001149)	$4.95	_____	_____
The Gospel of Luke: Jesus' Personal Touch—Study Guide (BWP001167)	$3.95	_____	_____
The Gospel of Luke: Jesus' Personal Touch—Large Print Study Guide (BWP001168)	$4.25	_____	_____
The Gospel of Luke: Jesus' Personal Touch—Teaching Guide (BWP001169)	$4.95	_____	_____
The Gospel of John: Light Overcoming Darkness, Part One—Study Guide (BWP001104)	$3.55	_____	_____
The Gospel of John: Light Overcoming Darkness, Part One—Large Print Study Guide (BWP001105)	$3.95	_____	_____
The Gospel of John: Light Overcoming Darkness, Part One—Teaching Guide (BWP001106)	$4.50	_____	_____
The Gospel of John: Light Overcoming Darkness, Part Two—Study Guide (BWP001109)	$3.55	_____	_____
The Gospel of John: Light Overcoming Darkness, Part Two—Large Print Study Guide (BWP001110)	$3.95	_____	_____
The Gospel of John: Light Overcoming Darkness, Part Two—Teaching Guide (BWP001111)	$4.50	_____	_____

The Book of Acts: Time to Act on Acts 1:8—Study Guide (BWP001142)	$3.95
The Book of Acts: Time to Act on Acts 1:8—Large Print Study Guide (BWP001143)	$4.25
The Book of Acts: Time to Act on Acts 1:8—Teaching Guide (BWP001144)	$4.95
The Corinthian Letters—Study Guide (BWP001121)	$3.55
The Corinthian Letters—Large Print Study Guide (BWP001122)	$4.25
The Corinthian Letters—Teaching Guide (BWP001123)	$4.95
Galatians and 1&2 Thessalonians—Study Guide (BWP001080)	$3.55
Galatians and 1&2 Thessalonians—Large Print Study Guide (BWP001081)	$3.95
Galatians and 1&2 Thessalonians—Teaching Guide (BWP001082)	$3.95
Letters to the Ephesians and Timothy—Study Guide (BWP001182)	$3.95
Letters to the Ephesians and Timothy—Large Print Study Guide (BWP001183)	$4.25
Letters to the Ephesians and Timothy—Teaching Guide (BWP001184)	$4.95
Hebrews and the Letters of Peter—Study Guide (BWP001162)	$3.95
Hebrews and the Letters of Peter—Large Print Study Guide (BWP001163)	$4.25
Hebrews and the Letters of Peter—Teaching Guide (BWP001164)	$4.95
Letters of James and John—Study Guide (BWP001101)	$3.55
Letters of James and John—Large Print Study Guide (BWP001102)	$3.95
Letters of James and John—Teaching Guide (BWP001103)	$4.25

Coming for use beginning March 2015

Exodus: Liberated for Life in Covenant with God—Study Guide (BWP001192)	$3.95
Exodus: Liberated for Life in Covenant with God—Large Print Study Guide (BWP001193)	$4.25
Exodus: Liberated for Life in Covenant with God—Teaching Guide (BWP001194)	$4.95

Standard (UPS/Mail) Shipping Charges*

Order Value	Shipping charge**	Order Value	Shipping charge**
$.01—$9.99	$6.50	$160.00—$199.99	$24.00
$10.00—$19.99	$8.50	$200.00—$249.99	$28.00
$20.00—$39.99	$9.50	$250.00—$299.99	$30.00
$40.00—$59.99	$10.50	$300.00—$349.99	$34.00
$60.00—$79.99	$11.50	$350.00—$399.99	$42.00
$80.00—$99.99	$12.50	$400.00—$499.99	$50.00
$100.00—$129.99	$15.00	$500.00—$599.99	$60.00
$130.00—$159.99	$20.00	$600.00—$799.99	$72.00**

Cost of items (Order value) _____

Shipping charges (see chart*) _____

TOTAL _____

*Please call 1-866-249-1799 if the exact amount is needed prior to ordering.

**For order values $800.00 and above, please call 1-866-249-1799 or check www.baptistwaypress.org

Please allow three weeks for standard delivery. For express shipping service: Call 1-866-249-1799 for information on additional charges.

YOUR NAME _____ PHONE _____

YOUR CHURCH _____ DATE ORDERED _____

SHIPPING ADDRESS _____

CITY _____ STATE _____ ZIP CODE _____

E-MAIL _____

MAIL this form with your check for the total amount to:
BAPTISTWAY PRESS, Baptist General Convention of Texas,
333 North Washington, Dallas, TX 75246-1798
(Make checks to "BaptistWay Press")

OR, **CALL** your order toll-free: 1-866-249-1799
(M-Fri 8:30 a.m.-5:00 p.m. central time).

OR, **E-MAIL** your order to: baptistway@texasbaptists.org.

OR, **ORDER ONLINE** at www.baptistwaypress.org.

We look forward to receiving your order! Thank you!